ARUNDEL PRIORY
1380-1980

ARUNDEL PRIORY

1380-1980
The College of the Holy Trinity

Mark Turnham Elvins

PHILLIMORE

1981

Published by
PHILLIMORE & CO. LTD.
London and Chichester

Head Office: Shopwyke Hall,
Chichester, Sussex, England

ISBN 0 85033 362 8

Printed and bound in Great Britain by
GARDEN CITY PRESS LTD.
Letchworth, Herts.

CONTENTS

LIST OF PLATES

(between pages 12 and 13)

I am honour bound to acknowledge my debt to the Duke of Norfolk and the Courtauld Institute for allowing me to publish photographs of the fine water colour pictures of the Fitzalan Chapel in the collection at Arundel Castle.

ACKNOWLEDGEMENTS

I am much obliged to Mr. Timothy McCann, Assistant Archivist of West Sussex, for his invaluable help in suggesting certain unpublished source material. I must also record my gratitude to Mr. John Brooke-Little, Norroy and Ulster King of Arms, not only for writing the Preface but also for encouraging me in the idea of writing this book. My sojourn at Arundel gave me ample scope for my researches and I must thank His Grace the Duke of Norfolk for supplying the Foreword and his Archivist Dr. John Martin Robinson for helping me track down some illusive details in Arundel Castle archives. Two brave ladies helped with the sometimes monotonous task of typing the manuscript, Mrs. Margaret Phillips and Miss Maisie Peachey to whom I extend my particular gratitude and my warmest thanks to Miss Evelyn G. Wedge for allowing me to consult her collection of books and letters. In fine I must admit the subject deserves perhaps a larger and more scholarly work but I hope the following pages will prove of interest or at least a cure for insomnia.

Dedicated to
Lady Mary Fitzalan-Howard
whose generosity has made this book possible.
Through her efforts, and those of
Sister Marie King,
Arundel Priory now fulfills
a new and Godly purpose

FOREWORD

Monastic property for the most part was redistributed at the Reformation to those who had engineered the demise of the religious orders; however, the following account describes not only the continuity of association between a monastic property and the founder's family, but also the eventual revival for religious use of the once dissolved property.

Unlike those who were paid in monastic land for their part in the Dissolution of the Monasteries, the 12th Earl of Arundel had to buy back his own family foundation from Henry VIII for the not inconsiderable sum of 1,000 marks. The 4th Earl and founder of Arundel College had intended it to be a place of prayer for himself and his ancestors, which the Chapel continues to be. Moreover, the canons of the College maintained a hospice for the elderly poor, and, in keeping with which the old College building is now devoted to a similar work. Thus history has come full circle and the pious wishes of a forebear continue to be fulfilled in new and vastly different circumstances.

MILES
XVII Duke of Norfolk

PREFACE

'Time hath his revolutions.' When Chief Justice Crew made this sententious remark in his judgement in the Earl of Oxford case in 1625, he referred to the solemn fact that there must be 'an end to all temporal things, *finis rerum* . . .'. Yet this same remark may aptly and more happily be applied to Arundel Priory. From time immemorial the Christian precept of charity was practised at Arundel under the patronage of the Earls of Arundel. Now, after the vicissitudes of centuries, the old buildings are once again being used for the care of the aged, thanks to the generous patronage of Lady Mary and Lady Sarah Fitzalan-Howard, descendants of the old Earls of Arundel. It is fitting, too, that the Order of Malta Homes Trust, which runs Arundel Priory, should have sprung from the oldest extant hospitaller Order in the world, the Order of St. John, perhaps better known as the Order of Malta, and that one of the trustees should be the present Earl of Arundel, Major-General the Duke of Norfolk. Time indeed hath its revolutions, but in this case they have gone full cycle.

It was a particularly happy thought of Father Mark Elvins to write a history of the Priory at this particular moment, when the new Alms Houses are almost ready to receive their first inmates. It is right that the history of the Priory should be recorded and I sincerely hope that it will be studied by all who have some concern with it.

It is a fascinating story, the very stuff of English social history, and Father Elvins has recorded it in a most appealing way. There runs through his narrative an obvious love of the place, engendered no doubt by his years as a priest of St. Philip's Cathedral, Arundel. Perhaps also there is another more intimate and so far unrecorded reason.

I will conclude these few words by telling the story of Father Elvins, the match-maker. It is a brief tale which also probably explains why he has done me the signal honour of asking me to write this preface. When I was Chancellor of the British Association of the Order of Malta, I was keen to involve the Association in the care of the aged and was actively looking for somewhere it could build alms houses or take over some moribund almshouse trust. Father Elvins, knowing of my quest and knowing also that the Priory was virtually unoccupied suggested that I get in touch with Lady Mary Fitzalan-Howard. This I did, with the result detailed above. By bringing us together Father Elvins has played an important role in the history of the Priory, a role which I acknowledge with gratitude.

J. P. BROOKE-LITTLE

Norroy and Ulster King of Arms

Knight Grand Cross of Grace and Devotion SMOM

INTRODUCTION

After six hundred years it is perhaps fitting that some record be made of the continuing fortunes of a beautiful and historic complex of medieval buildings, known originally as Arundel College.

To contemporary minds colleges are to do with universities or schools, at least they are generally considered places of education. However, originally a college was simply a corporate body, founded for the service of the Church, and thus invariably made up of a substantial body of clerics. Their duty was to provide for the celebration of the liturgy—the singing of the divine office in choir and the offering of daily Mass. As such, colleges of this kind were an integral part of Medieval Catholicism.

It was not until the latter part of the Middle Ages that Colleges appeared with a specifically educational purpose— such were the University Colleges of Oxford and Cambridge and the schools of Eton and Winchester. There were also other types of 'College', for instance, the bodies of men who served Cathedral Churches: viz., Colleges of Chaplains or minor canons.

In some cases the Colleges would run a grammar school— the clergy deriving their income from chantry service. Arundel College provided for education in a small way, but like some other colleges also served the needs of the aged poor, in maintaining the Hospice of the Holy Trinity (or Maison Dieu). The fourth Earl of Arundel in founding the College and Hospice, moreover, had in mind his and his family's need of salvation, and thus he endowed the College for the perpetual offering of Mass for the repose of the souls of his family and his ancestors. To this day Mass is still offered for all buried in the College (Fitzalan) Chapel. The College can thus be described as a 'Chantry College'.

The charitable purpose of the College's hospice has been recently revived, the College (Priory) itself becoming a home for the aged under the patronage of the Earl's descendants and the Sovereign, Military and Hospitaller Order of St. John.

Chapter I

THE EARLIEST RECORDED FOUNDATIONS

THE BUILDINGS as they have survived into the 20th century constitute the remains of a college for secular canons, which include a chapel, the Master's House and part of the cloister. This college was founded in 1380 to provide for a body of secular clergy to offer Masses for the founder and his family and provide for the needs of the parish. Before 1085 there was already a similar foundation in existence in Arundel and is referred to in the Domesday Book as constituting the 'clerks of St. Nicholas',[1] who served the parish church of Arundel of that dedication. From such records it would appear that this foundation was the earliest to be recorded on the site. However, before 1094[2] provision had been made for this body of secular clergy in Arundel parish church to be suppressed, and a Benedictine priory subject to the Abbey of Seez in Normandy to be founded in its place.

From the little that is known of the body of secular clergy attached to Arundel parish church before the Domesday record, it would seem that it resembled a college of secular canons, similar in type, although not in detail to the minor canons attached to certain cathedrals. Mentioned together with the parochial church of St. Nicholas in Domesday is the chapel of St. Martin[3] in Arundel Castle keep. However 'the parochial church may, in all probability, claim the precedence in point of antiquity, as it certainly must in importance, and extent of possession'. This latter was endowed with a permanent revenue of 24 shillings, derived from the customs of the borough, together with 25 hides of land, in the manor of South Harting.[4] Of this foundation not a vestige now remains.

1

With the upheavals that followed the Norman Conquest, much of England was divided up among the Conqueror's followers. One of the principal recipients was Roger de Montgomery, who commanded the main body of the Norman army at Hastings. This Roger, subsequent to the Conquest, was granted among many other lands and titles the Earldom of Arundel. He immediately proceeded to repair and fortify the Castle of Arundel; he moreover enlarged the town and elevated it to the dignity of a borough,[5] and made provision for the foundation of a Benedictine Priory attached to the parish church. He had already restored the Abbey of St. Martin de Seez in Normandy, and this was to become the mother house of Arundel Priory. The new foundation was therefore to be a dependency, but it was not until shortly before Earl Roger's death in 1094 that a grant was made, enabling building to commence. The Earl also gave other lands, advowsons and possessions to provide for the Priory's support. The erection of the building, however, was slow, largely as a consequence of the war-like activities of Earl Roger's successors Hugh Montgomery and Robert-called Bellesme (after his mother's inheritance). By 1102 the house was at last ready for occupation, but not before the property had been forfeit to the Crown, through the brigandage of Robert Bellesme (2nd Earl). In the event King Henry gave his patronage to the new Priory and four monks and a prior were despatched from the Abbey of Seez to take up residence. Gratian[6] was the name of the first prior appointed by the Abbot of Seez, and under him the monks enjoyed a quiet and uneventful existence.

The honours and estates of Arundel having become forfeit to the Crown, King Henry I bestowed them on his Queen Adeliza. Upon Henry's death in 1135, Adeliza conveyed them by marriage to her second husband William D'Albini to become the 1st Earl of Arundel of his line. This Earl died in 1176[7] and was succeeded by his son, also William. Heretofore the Priory had existed at a distance from the parish church, but in 1178 the rectory of Arundel falling vacant, the new Earl sought to annex the Priory to the service of the parish church.[8] The old priory building was thus abandoned and the rectory (on the site of the present castle car park) was adapted for use by the Prior and his monks, and became known as the Priory of St. Nicholas. An interesting sidelight into the life of the Priory is given by Ralph, Bishop of Chichester, in his ordinance of *c.* 1216.

> Also we command that the chancell dore of the quire of the said monks, from the end of the great masse, unto the first hower of the day following, to be shutt by their sacrist; and the outward dores of the church to be shutt by the said vicar, or by his beneficed clerk sworne, soe that the wandering monks goe not out, at their pleasure, to behold the vanities of this world.[9]

The priors continued to be appointed by the Abbot of Seez, with the approbation of the community, and were in turn instituted by the Bishop of Chichester. Part of the ceremony of induction of a new prior consisted of his acknowledging the patronage of the Earl and in token of this declared himself the Earl's orator and chaplain. The relationship between the Priory and its patron was not without certain misunderstandings. One of the Earls had requested certain prayers to be made by the monks in the Priory church, but Prior Nicholas rejected his request wholeheartedly on the grounds that they owed their patron no such service. The Earl, understandably irritated, demanded to know by what title they held the Priory church, the poor monks could find no document to support their position. Encouraged by the monks' dilemma, the Earl insisted upon unqualified acceptance of his patronage. The spiritual life of the Priory, needless to say, suffered considerably and there was resort to 'strife and brawling'. The case was finally submitted to the decision of the Bishop of Chichester, who pronounced the following decree:

> That the said religious, the prior of Arundell, and monks, and their successors, cause to be devoutlie cellebrated amongst them, by turne, by the moneth, one Masse for the soules of the Earls of Arundell, deceased of whose names it shall and will lawfully apeare; another Masse for the Earle living, for the time being, by fifteen daies; and that the said church of Arundell, with all the rights to the rectory or parsonage of the same belonging, may fully remayne, and bee for ever hereafter, to the said religious, the Prior of Arundell and monks and their successors, appropriated, to be possessed to their owne uses, except the great tithes of the land underwritten, assigned to the augmenting of such vicaridy. And the same church of Arundell to them, of our liberallity, wee doe appropriat, saving the perpetuall vicaridy in the church afforesaid.[10]

Despite this ruling of the Bishop further quarrels were to break out between the monks and their erstwhile patron, and the brethren proved dilatory in the performance of their duties to their patron as well as to their mother house in Normandy. A common seal was devised for the community, and under this authority the Prior bought and sold land to the Priory's benefit, even bestowing a manor on the Bishop of Chichester—perhaps a tactful move in the circumstances.

The tide of history was destined, however, to overtake the little Priory of Arundel. As an alien priory, subject to a French abbey, it had already been confiscated by Edward II in 1325, and was to experience similar predicaments a few years later at the outbreak of the Hundred Years War. Edward III was on the throne and his French wars were proving disastrous to the national coffers, a situation in which a French mother house was a cause of acute embarrassment. Inevitably, Edward III decided to levy a tax on all alien priories for the relief of his military operations. This took immediate and drastic effect, and over a period of 23 years resulted in plundering and confiscation. Arundel Priory had the security of being independent and self-supporting, and the fact that any ties with France had been reduced to a nominal character now proved to be a great advantage in reducing the risk of wholesale plunder.

Arundel Priory was once more in royal custody by the 27 July 1337.[11] In fact, all alien houses remained in the king's keeping until about 16 February 1361. However, by 1 December 1369 the Priory had been taken into royal hands once more and thus it remained for a period of over 11 years.[12]

When Edward III confiscated Arundel Priory in 1337, the keeping of the house was committed to the prior in return for a farm of £35, rented yearly to the king. The prior had to find for the monks and the servants of the house in providing their sustenance and the usual stipends, and had to meet the sundry other expenses incumbent on the Priory. By 1340 the farm dues from the Prior to Arundel were reduced to £27 a year. This commitment was to continue 'during the royal pleasure'. On 11 June that same year, licence was given to the Priory to acquire, in mortmain, land and rent to the value of 60s. yearly, despite alien status. In 1342[13] the commitment to the Prior was allowed to continue for the duration of the war provided that the Priory remained in the king's hands. Despite this, by the 20 March 1349 the Priory had been reduced to such poverty that the buildings had become dilapidated with no visible means to effect their restoration; thus the farm dues of 40 marks were reduced to 20 marks annually.

In the midst of these distressing financial problems the Priory had been visited with yet another affliction. A dreadful pestilence, originating in India, had spread to Europe, and having swept through Italy across the Alps into France, from whence in the autumn of 1348 it was brought to England.[14] From the port of Southampton it quickly spread to Sussex, where ordinary business, as a result, was brought to a standstill. So virulent was the pestilence that victims often died within a few hours, and animals died in their thousands. Those who escaped infection only lived on to experience the dreadful famine that followed. Such was the fate of the monks of Arundel Priory, and even after a year when the disease had taken its course they found their farmers and servants so decimated that the Priory lands remained untilled and what crops survived had already rotted. The lack of a fresh supply of husbandmen threatened the Priory's very existence. Under the pressure of famine and war tax the monks resolved to present their plight to Robert Stratford, Bishop of Chichester, hoping that his intervention would enable them to obtain more profitable lands. In the event the Bishop offered them the perpetual advowson of the parish church of Rustington and promised to invest them with the appropriation of the said church together with those of Kirdford and Littlehampton, whose patronage the Priory already held. This offer was made in return for the Priory lands and rents in the parishes of Slinfold, Wisborough, Rudgwick, Horsham, Kirdford, Warnham and Billingshurst. The Bishop moreover did his best to obtain royal licence on the Priory's behalf, and on 24 June 1352 King Edward signed a patent, authorising this exchange and granting the monks the rights of appropriation. There was, however, an unaccountable delay of nearly two years before the deed was actually signed by each of the contracting parties in February of 1353. The assignment from the Bishop of the churches of

Rustington, Kirdford and Littlehampton followed in June, and their rents and profits were made over to the Priory *in toto*.

This change in fortune nearly doubled the revenues of the Priory and with the additional grants of the churches of Yapton, Billingshurst and Cocking, prosperity returned once more to the little community. Moreover, with the peaceful conclusion to the French campaigns in 1360 the king cancelled the levy of war tax on the Priory.[15] However, within ten years the French wars were resumed and the tax (20 marks), amounting to about one-fifth of the Priory's revenues, was reimposed.

Chapter II

THE FOUNDATION OF THE COLLEGE OF THE HOLY TRINITY

THE DOMESDAY RECORD mentions the existence of a chapel of St. Martin in the keep at Arundel Castle, no doubt owing its dedication to the mother house of Arundel Priory—the Abbey of St. Martin de Seez in Normandy. This chapel was formerly situated over the entrance to the keep, but all that remains as evidence of its existence is one solitary window.[1] This chapel was served by one chaplain (whose annual income was £4 in 1272 [Domesday mentions 12 pence][2]), who was appointed by the Earl of Arundel. By 1275 this chapel in the keep had been superseded by the chapel of St. George in the south-eastern part of the castle (the part now known as the dining room). In 1344 a bull was obtained from Pope Clement VI by Richard Fitzalan (third Earl of his line) for the endowment of a perpetual chantry for three priests in the parochial church of St. Nicholas (then owned by the Priory). However, the convenient proximity of the chapel of St. George caused the Earl to request yet another bull authorising the transfer of this foundation to the castle chapel. This granted, the Earl, having grown rich in the French wars, sought to enlarge his foundation to the status of a college. To this end a bull was obtained from Pope Innocent VI[3] in 1354.

The establishment of this college may have all the appearance of the pious wishes of a generous benefactor, but it was somewhat accelerated by the third Earl's domestic situation. The plain fact is that he wished the annulment of his marriage to Isobel Despenser, whom he had married at the tender age of 16, at the behest of his father, Edmund, second Earl of Arundel, in 1321. After 24 years of untroubled marriage he thus petitioned the Pope for annulment, on the grounds of it having been contracted during his minority and that he only accepted the contract out of respect for his father, having been 'forced by blows to cohabit'! No matter how unconvincing his claim and despite a son and two daughters[4] by the marriage, the Earl's petition was granted without hesitation in 1344.[5] The Pope ordered the Archbishop of Canterbury and the Bishop of Chichester to make enquiries and to act according to Canon Law. Presumably unbeknown to the authorities, Earl Richard had already struck up an an illicit liaison with Eleanor Beaumont, widow of John Beaumont and daughter of Henry, Earl of Lancaster, and no doubt herein lay the real motive for his actions.

Despite what must be taken as flagrant adultery nothing was allowed to impede the proposed match. The Earl secretly married Eleanor Beaumont on 5 February 1345, but for them to remain legally married it was necessary to obtain a papal dispensation, because of the relationship[6] between Eleanor and the Earl's previous wife, Isobel; Pope Clement VI granted the necessary dispensation on condition that Earl Richard found three chaplaincies within a year, each of the annual value of 10 marks to be attached to the parish of Arundel.[7]

It was later discovered that Richard and Eleanor were also related and so a new dispensation was necessary. This dispensation required chaplaincies to be founded in Arundel Castle in addition to those already stipulated.[8] Earl Richard decided to make the most of these stipulations and accordingly obtained from Pope Innocent in 1354[9] the licence to found, with the wealth he had amassed in the French wars, what was to be subsequently known as a College of Secular Canons. This college originally was to consist of an unspecified number of priests and clerks, attached to the Castle Chapel of St. George, and the Bishops of Winchester, Rochester and St. Asaph were instructed by Pope Innocent to promulgate the statutes.[10]

The establishment of this college was never to be completed in Earl Richard's lifetime, but his appointment of three chaplains to serve the Chapel of St. George had already displayed his grand sense of liturgy. The Earl did not waver in his intentions of founding a college, however, despite the delay of

20 years, for six months before his death in 1376 he obtained a royal licence on 20 July 1375[11] for his manors of Angmering, Wepham and Warningcamp to provide a yearly rent of 107 marks for the maintenance of a number of clerks and chaplains in the service of the chantry in 'his chapel of Arundel'. This rent was to continue until the chantry was endowed with lands of equivalent value. Licence was also granted to acquire such lands and convey them as the inalienable property of the clerks and chaplains.[12]

On the 24 January 1376 the Earl died, but in his will he instructed his executors to proceed with the establishment of his proposed foundation. The will left no doubt as to the purpose of this foundation, which was for the noteworthy daily celebration of the Divine Office in his chapel at Arundel Castle. Moreover, prayers were to be offered for the souls of his father, mother, wife and children, their descendants and all Christian people, and Masses were to be offered at the behest of the executors. To this end he left 1,000 marks to acquire the necessary land endowments of equivalent value to the aforementioned rents. In the will he stipulated that the community should reside in the north bailey or Beaumont Tower (keep);[13] that they should rise in summer at sunrise and in winter at the break of day.[14]

Richard, son of the third Earl's second wife, succeeded to the title and as one of his late father's executors obtained on 16 March 1378 letters patent giving him power to grant a further 95 marks annually in addition to the existing 107 marks left by his father. This additional revenue was taken from the Earl's manors of Peppering, South Stoke, Tortington and Upmarden, and was to be paid to the new foundation until such time as he could grant lands and tenements of an equal yearly value.[15]

The original intention had been to establish the college in the Chapel of St. George in the castle, but in November 1379 the venue was switched to the now ailing Priory. Edward III, by taxing the Priory's revenues for his foreign wars, had impoverished its resources, despite the increase in its possessions. The parish church was still the Priory church, but the Priory was practically deserted and rapidly falling into decay.[16]

The administration of the sacraments was more than likely left to the good will of the neighbouring clergy; the monks had for the most part fled the desolate spot for the refuge of the mother house (the Abbey of Seez in Normandy). All this had not escaped Earl Richard's notice, who, considering the peaceful occupation and intended permanence of his college foundation, had decided not to establish it within the castle walls, in case in the event of a successful military assault it suffered the inevitable desecration. Thus the destitute Priory and the wants of the parish church suggested an alternative location, where once the Benedictine monks had followed their calling. This situation, removed from the military pre-occupation of the castle, ensured a measure of immunity from any warlike enterprise.[17]

The Priory, however, was still in existence and the parish church was still the Priory church. Accordingly on 11 November 1379, as recorded among the letters patent, is a protection order for Richard Macheby, Northampton Herald,[18] and for two yeomen for safe escort to the Abbey of Seez to obtain the Abbot's licence for a foundation of a chantry within the parish church. By Easter of 1380 it was resolved not merely to found a chantry, but a chantry college, occupying the entire Priory— which would have to be accordingly annulled. Earl Richard having thus determined on secularising the Priory and uniting it with his proposed foundation next proceeded to secure royal approbation.[19]

In Easter week of 1380[20] an inquisition was held at Arundel to determine if the proposed foundation would be to the prejudice of the king or any other party. The Earl proposed to dissolve the Priory and annex its revenues to those intended for the college, and place the rectory of the parish church in the possession of the master of the college. To accommodate the said master and his chaplains he proposed to build a suitable edifice upon the site of the existing Priory, and add five secular chaplains to the six already named in his late father's will, and to this add two more to make a complement of thirteen. Notwithstanding this substantial number the Earl proposed the further addition of deacons and subdeacons, clerks and other officers, dedicating the whole foundation to the Holy Trinity, the Blessed Virgin Mary and all the saints.[21]

As a result of this inquisition one difficulty arose. Back in 1243 Hugh D'Albini, Earl of Arundel, died leaving four married sisters as heirs. Thus his property had to be divided among these ladies and their descendants. One of the sisters, Isobel, had married John Fitzalan, Lord of Clun and Oswaldestre, by whom she had a son, John. He succeeded his uncle Hugh in possession of Arundel Castle and the earldom in 1243,[22] but the advowson of the Priory passed to another of the four sisters, Cecily, who was married to Roger de Monte Alto. The advowson had subsequently, with the rest of Roger de Monte Alto's possessions, passed to his kinsman Robert de Morley who had alienated his inheritance to Queen Isobel, wife of King Edward II. From her it had passed to her son King Edward III, who had granted it to his eldest son Prince Edward (the Black Prince) and thus was inherited by his son King Richard II.

This advowson amounted to nothing more than nominal possession of the Priory; it did not confer the right of presentation to the rectory for that was held by the Prior, and the power of choosing the Prior was possessed by the Abbot and convent of Seez.[23] This advowson had been constantly challenged by the Earls of Arundel, who claimed it should be theirs as an attachment to their demesne. Moreover, the jurors at the inquisition were unwilling to swear that the advowson had been assigned to Roger Monte Alto as no mention of this was made in the disposal of the inheritance. What is more, there was no documentary evidence which recorded the possessor of Arundel Priory,[24] and King Richard as his heir was determined to turn the situation to his advantage. Thus until his possession of the advowson was recognised he refused to grant a licence for the incorporation of the college. Earl Richard had met his match. In order to obtain the licence for his proposed foundation he had, he discovered, not only to relinquish his claim on the advowson, but also pay a sum of £40[25] as compensation for the annual fine of 20 marks which the Priory was subject to in times of war. In return the king would grant him the advowson, provided another advowson worth not less than £20 and with a taxable value of 21 marks was made over to him within the space of three years—on pain of a fine of £1,000.

On 1 April 1380[26] King Richard conceded the licence (see Appendix I) and the advowson was assigned to the Earl of Arundel and his heirs—in consideration of his ancestors who founded the Priory. The king's patent moreover included authorisation for the dissolution of the convent and the foundation of a college for a master and 12 chaplains and granted possession of the former Priory for this purpose. This, of course, was dependent on the assent of the Abbot of Seez, which once procured should finally relinquish any interest the Abbey of St. Martin of Seez might have in the said property. The Abbot raised no difficulties, indeed he was most obliging considering how much his poor little community had suffered before they finally retraced their steps to Normandy.

By the same letters patent the possession of the Priory was assigned to the Earl, together with licence to found a chantry in the old parish church, and endow the college with the annulled property of the Priory. The Abbot and Convent of Seez remitted their rights to the master and chaplains of the college, who thus took possession. The Bishop of Chichester granted his licence for the offering of Mass on the 24 May 1380,[27] being the feast of Corpus Christi, and as such must be regarded as the foundation day.

To conclude his transactions the industrious Earl next petitioned the papacy to ensure there was approval all round. The Abbot and Convent of Seez had already asked papal approval for assigning the Priory to the Earl. In July 1380 a Papal Mandate was sent to the Bishop of Chichester stating that if all the circumstances regarding the intended foundation were as stated, the Bishop was to receive from the Abbot and Convent of Seez the resignation of the Priory and was to give the Earl licence to institute the College of Canons.[28]

Building commenced. The site of the Priory was on an eminence adjoining the south side of the old parish church. The Priory buildings were demolished together with the old parish church, and to this day the only masonry definitely identified with the Priory lies in the vaults of the new church making up the structure of one of the stone coffins.[29] The fourth Earl's building thus commenced with a vengeance. The new college site was extended beyond the Priory's original boun-

Prospect of
ARRVNDELL CA=
stle & Towne, y.° West-
side

1. The town of Arundel in 1644, from an engraving by Wenceslaus Hollar.

2. The 4th and founding Earl of Arundel seen holding the Fitzalan Chapel in miniature, taken from the east window of the Fitzalan Chapel

3. (*right*) Adam de Eartham the first master of the College of the Holy Trinity at Arundel, 1380-1382.

Sit adm Ertham pm mestre d'cest College gist pcy dieuç de s'alme eyt mcy amen

4. (*below*) The cenotaph of the 3rd Earl of Arundel (the father of the founder) and his countess, rescued from the Cluniac Priory of Lewes at its dissolution and placed in Chichester Cathedral.

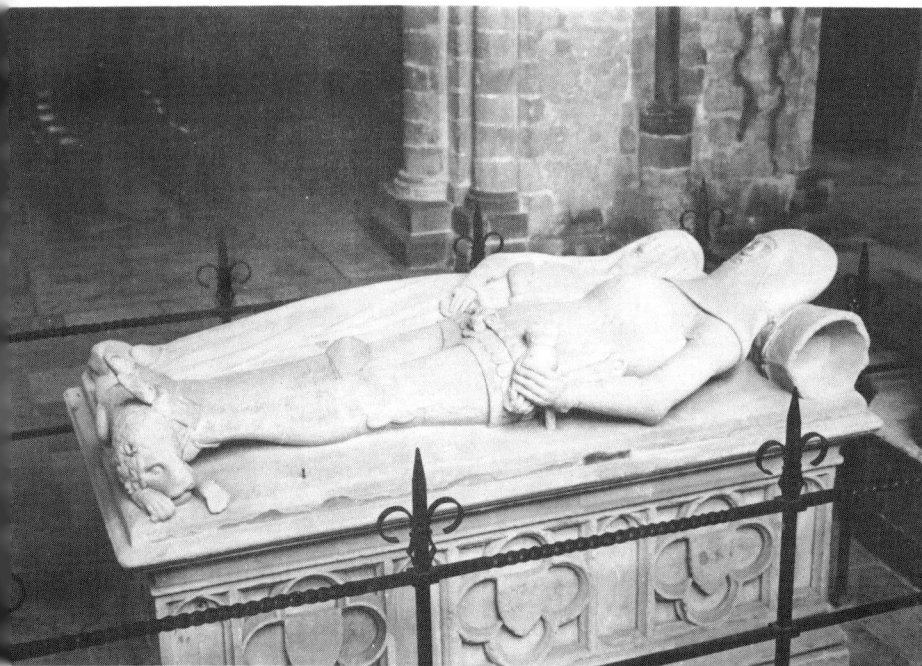

5. Interior of Fitzalan Chapel, early this century.

6. Arundel Priory, showing the Fitzalan Chapel from the south side; in the foreground is the mortuary chapel of the 14th Duke of Norfolk.

7. Exterior of the Priory from the London Road.

8. Priory buildings from inside the quadrangle.

9. An artist's impression of the scene of desolation in the Fitzalan Chapel after Sir William Waller's troops had recaptured Arundel Castle in 1644.

10. The condition of the Fitzalan Chapel after its ceiling had been dismantled in 1782.

11. (*right*) Another view of the Fitzalan Chapel showing further deterioration.

12. Bernard Marmaduke, 16th Duke of Norfolk and 27th Earl of Arundel, 1908-1975, from his monument recently erected in the Fitzalan Chapel.

daries and lacked no financial endowment to ensure an edifice worthy of the time and energy expended by its founder. As a college it was accordingly built on a quadrangle, surrounding an open court, partly occupied by cloisters. To the north arose the new Collegiate Chapel, forming a chancel to the new parish church, on the east the refectory and the kitchens, and the master's house, a rectangular structure, was placed against the south-east corner of the chapel, with a communicating door and flight of steps to his private chapel. The rest of the quadrangle was given over to the accommodation of the secular canons, deacons, subdeacons and clerks, etc. The entrance into the quadrangle was through a great gateway at the south-west corner which still affords access to the existing buildings to this day.

The gateway became a famous landmark for reasons other than its size and convenience, for upon its great doors hung a 'Sanctuary Ring'. A fugitive fleeing a hue and cry (which was the ancient way of running a criminal to earth) could claim the rights of sanctuary once he grasped the ring of the door (*cf.* the 'Sanctuary knocker' at Durham and the 'frith-stool' at Hexham, which operated on the same principle). The rights of sanctuary were given by ecclesiastical authority to fugitives from justice who had taken refuge in a church and were thus afforded safe custody, provided they took an oath of abjuration before a coroner and proceeded to a seaport within 40 days. If within this time the fugitive refused to comply he could be removed by the local justices.

In 1404 one John Mott was committed to prison in Arundel Castle on a charge of robbery. He made good his escape, but was discovered. Immediately a hue and cry (a posse of local townsmen) gave chase. John Mott made straight for the new-found college and grasped the 'Sanctuary Ring' on the great gate, but to no avail. The constable, ignoring the rights of sanctuary, took him briskly back to his castle cell. As a result of this violation of sanctuary the constable was sentenced to be cudgelled five times through the church of Arundel. However, this was commuted to offering a lighted candle at High Mass the following Sunday, as it was discovered that the constable having at last realised his mistake took John Mott straight back to the church.[30]

Chapter III

THE COLLEGE LIFE BEGINS

BY THE END OF 1381 the building of the college was so advanced that the canons had already taken up occupation. On 7 December 1381 the Earl as empowered by royal licence assigned to the college 107 marks of rent from the manors of Angmering, Wepham and Warningcamp, which his late father (the third Earl) had been licensed to grant to the originally-proposed foundation within the castle. The Earl also conveyed the 97 marks of rent from the manors of Peppering, South Stoke and Tortington which he himself had been licensed to grant in 1378 as an additional endowment to the same foundation, before the decision to move the site of the Priory. This total of 204 marks of rent was however only to be assigned until property of an equivalent annual value could be bestowed on the college.[1]

While the college's buildings peacefully rose above the ancient monastic site the rest of England was in turmoil. The year 1381 saw the occupation of the college in a country torn by the 'Peasants Revolt', in which the port of Arundel was to play its part. The Black Death of 30 years before had so reduced the population that the fields were not tilled and the nation's economy was in ruins. To re-coup the losses to the royal exchequer a Poll Tax was imposed, and it was this which caused the south-eastern counties to rise in open revolt.

Despite the evil times the second master's (William White) account rolls for the college's financial year Michaelmas 1382 to Michaelmas 1383[2] show nothing of the strictures inflicted on most of southern Entland, apart from 'arrears' being brought forward from the year before. What is more, during the entire year of 1382-83 the college had its full complement of master, 12 canons and others besides.

14

On 11 February 1383 the Earl of Arundel assigned to King Richard the manor of Sevenhampton in Somerset, which the king accepted in lieu of the advowson the Earl had promised to convey within the space of three years with an equivalent annual value of not less than £20 per annum and with a taxable value of 21 marks.[3] Thus the Earl fulfilled the obligations of the licence he had obtained for the foundation of his college. The master and the canons of the college were accordingly released from the annual payment of 20 marks levied by the crown since the French Wars.

The statutes for the government of the college were not drawn up until December 1387.[4] By this time it must be concluded that the buildings were almost complete and thus the statutes were deemed a necessary conclusion to over six years of bustling and noisy activity. The statutes relate how the college came to be founded, as already stated, and record the founder's pious wishes for his own immortality and that the prayers of the community might secure the same, together with that of the deceased members of his family. The statutes state the college was to possess 13 chaplains, or secular priests (known as secular canons), two deacons, two subdeacons, two acolytes and four choristers. All were permitted to leave the community, not being bound like a religious order, and thus were under no vow of poverty and could therefore hold property and could quit when they pleased, provided notice was given of not less than three months.

One was to be chosen from among the clergy of the community to be the master or 'custos' of the college, another was to be chosen as 'sub-master' to act in the master's absence. The precentor was chosen to supervise the ordering of the choir and another canon was to be elected master of choristers (one of the number could also be elected bursar), and there were also to be lay-sacrists. The master was to be the appointee of the patron who would select from two candidates previously elected and presented by the community. The clergy of the said community had to meet within 15 days to elect two of their number, or two outsiders. The Earl's candidate was then to be presented to the Bishop of Chichester (or his representative) and subsequently instituted with letters from the Bishop.

If the Earl failed to nominate, the appointment fell to the Bishop. The new master took an oath on the Gospels, in the presence of the community, to uphold his office and obey the statutes. The entire college was to take an oath of obedience to the master, and to the sub-master for when he acted on his behalf. The master was to be in sole charge of the maintenance of the establishment, keeping inventories of its possessions (see Appendix II) and looking after its interests. He was also to be responsible for upholding the college laws, supervising the interests and comforts of its brethren, and presenting an inspiring example to all in his charge. The master was appointed confessor to all the brethren, and was responsible for hearing their confessions at the appointed seasons of Advent, Lent and Whitsuntide (appointing one of the clergy to hear his own).

It was to be the master's right to appoint the sub-master; having first been nominated by the college he likewise took an oath. He was to be more than just the master's assistant, for when occasion demanded he was to be his delegate, and during an interregnum, owing to the death or retirement of the master, he was to take on full responsibilities, with authority to correct or condone the behaviour and activities of the brethren. In the ordinary course of events his duties would involve no more than supervision of the library and charge of the vestments, plate and other valuables; in his ordinary capacity he also had responsibility for the time of the daily office and providing what was necessary for Holy Mass. Statutes specify five household servants: a butler, a baker, two boys, and a groom for the Master's horse. If there was a death among the clergy a replacement had to be found within three months.

The Earl had moreover introduced safeguards into the statutes against the decay and decline in religious character experienced by the previous foundation. He stipulated that the institution's aim was the support and execution of divine worship. The constant residence of the canons was insisted upon as was their regular attendance in choir, in an attempt to safeguard against the deficiences of the Priory in its latter years. To enforce this ruling permission to officiate in neighbouring churches was restricted to occasions of real necessity, and then only with the master's permission. Any absentee from divine office was to be fined accordingly.

The brethren were to be in choir 'at sunrise' in summertime and at 'break of day' in wintertime.[5] The day was to begin with Matins, followed by the office of Lauds and Prime, after which followed the conventual Mass. The daily Mass was to be sung by one of the canons at the high altar of the conventual chapel, each of the 12 priest brethren taking on the duty for a week in turn, during which week he was to be designated 'hebdomadarius'. After the daily conventual Mass the brethren recited the office of Terce and Sext, which alternated with the private Masses at the other altars and chantries around the chapel and so was to continue up to the hour of noon, when the office of None was to be said. During the course of the afternoon the sub-master would again summon the community to choir for Vespers and Compline. Whatever leisure this round of prayer afforded was to be taken up with improving study such as that of Holy Scripture.

The founder's will, as outlined in the statutes, insisted that the brethren be clad simply in the same manner and that they should dine together and do all things conveniently in common. Meals were to be taken together and no permission would be given for dining outside the refectory, except in cases of bodily infirmity. There were to be two tables in the refectory, 'High' and 'Low'. A bell was to ring to summon to dinner, supper or collation, and at the main meals as a remedy for arguments there would be readings from Holy Scripture or one of the Fathers. On other occasions any conversation was to be of a useful nature, preferably in Latin. Women were to be introduced into the college only on rare occasions, and then only when considered legitimate. It was considered unseemly, particularly for priests, to go out alone; therefore their recreation should be in pairs so as to ensure propriety of behaviour and a shield from worldly concourse.[6] Only the master could be absent from the college; the rest of the brethren had to be in continuous residence, including the sub-master, priests and clerks. They could, with permission of the master or sub-master, be absent for a short time, but unlike other chantry colleges the statutes make no allowance for vacations. Priests could only visit neighbouring churches for a legitimate reason, such as the obsequies of a benefactor. None could venture out at night except to visit the sick. If a guest were bidden to a meal in the refectory, the member of the college introducing him had to pay 2d. for a meal at high table, but 1d. if at the lower table. The charge could be paid on the occasion or be deducted from the member's stipend. However, if the person invited was the guest of the college the charge was to be paid from the common fund. The consent for receiving personal guests was not usually to be extended beyond a duration of three days without permission from the master.[7]

Members of the college were forbidden to gamble within the precincts, within the parish, or anywhere for that matter. No hunting dogs were to be kept in the college, and members of the community were only permitted to go hunting in the company of 'honest persons' and then only outside the times of Divine Office. Otherwise the brethren were to spend their leisure in reading the Scriptures or in some 'honest task'.[8]

If any of the canons fell sick or became senile, they were to continue to receive bodily and financial sustenance and in whatever portion was deemed necessary. In the case of infirmity among the clerks or choristers the master, in consultation with the clergy, would decide whether to keep them on.[9]

The college chapter would be expected to decide on whether any member had committed a breach of discipline and enquiry would be made into whether there was need for correction. The chapter (made up of the master and the canons) would investigate any member suspected of a crime. In the case of murder the culprit would no longer remain in Orders and had to be expelled. In cases of adultery, incest, rape, sacrilege, false witness or theft, if the guilty party confessed to the master and the fellows of the college, he would be permitted to stay on after he had received due correction. However, he was also to be bound to an oath never to commit the crime again on pain of expulsion. On the other hand, any member found guilty of fornication, rebellion, quarrelling, drunkenness, or even greed, was to be rebuked, and on the second offence, to be expelled as a hopeless case of iniquity.[10]

There was no right of appeal, but if after 40 days no punishment was given by the master or sub-master, the local bishop was to intervene. In the case of the master misbehaving, his fellows were to upbraid him, and if he still failed to mend his ways, after two warnings he was to be denounced to the bishop.[11]

The community was expected to dress as befitted their situation and no extraordinary clothing was to be countenanced. The outer garments of the clergy were to be of full material with buttoned sleeves; their footwear was to be without pointed toes, and their general appearance was to bespeak of gravity. Each member of the college had to conform to certain sartorial regulations. The master, sub-master and canons were to wear cloth of the same cut and should appear dressed in like manner particularly on great feasts. The clerks could wear garments of the same cut, but of different colour, or they could wear a shorter tunic. The shape and cut of clothing was to be decided by the master and the cost provided by the members' stipends.[12]

The canons in choir were to wear surplices with black copes (Cappa nigra) and black fur almuces, as according to the Sarum use. On a canon's appointment this choir dress was provided by the munificence of the founder, but any subsequent new garment had to be paid for out of the common fund as part of the canon's stipend. Clerks and choristers were to wear surplices and black copes in the same way (without the almuce which was a distinguishing mark of those in Holy Orders).

On 5 February 1386 the Earl obtained licence to endow the college with property in lieu of the 100-marks rent which had been previously assigned.[13] By 1387 the Earl had completed the statutes for his college and they were accordingly submitted for the approval of the Bishop of Chichester, one Thomas Rushook, who duly approved them on 1 December 1387.[14] However, the Earl retained the right of changing, deleting or adding any detail to the statutes, as he saw fit, and claimed the right of placing his own interpretation on what was contained therein. The Earl also declared that no alteration was to be made contrary to the spirit of the foundation.

Chapter IV

COLLEGE PERSONNEL

IN THE COLLEGE STATUTES the sub-master was to be appointed by the master from among the chaplains and was bound to take an oath similar to that taken by the master and like the master had to ensure that the statutes were upheld by the rest of the community.[1] The succentor-sacrist was also selected from among the chaplains, but if it was deemed necessary to appoint a bursar he was to be appointed by the common vote of the community, and could be any chaplain excluding the master, sub-master, and succentor.[2]

One of the chaplains was to be appointed by the master as head of the choristers, and all other chaplains, deacons, sub-deacons, acolytes and lay choristers were to be admitted by the master in consultation with the senior or wiser members of the community.[3] Any vacancy occurring among the chaplaincies, as a result of death, resignation or dismissal, had to be filled within three months, or the appointment would lapse to the local ordinary (bishop).[4] On their appointment the chaplains had to swear in the presence of the master and the community[5] to uphold the statutes of the college. They also had to swear obedience to the master, and in his absence to the sub-master. All the deacons, sub-deacons and acolytes had similarly to swear obedience,[6] but the choristers were simply expected to obey out of respect for their seniors. Most of the appointments were not limited to the college personnel, thus if there was no suitable candidate in the community for a certain post, one could be selected from outside. However, the posts of sub-master, succentor, bursar and choirmaster were always given to existing members of the community.

The statutes were quite specific about the appointment of choristers. They had to have reached 10 years of age, and be poor, honest and teachable, particularly in doctrine and manners. Moreover, they had to be well suited to the life.

Up to the account roll of 1459-60 there is also mention of three valets and two boys. After this date there is also mention of a butler, a baker, a cook, an under-baker, and an under-cook.[7]

The Masters

Adam Ertham

The surviving evidence of the existence of this master is his brass in the college chapel. The inscription beneath (since removed) read as follows:

> Sir Ad'm Ertham p'm'estr d'cest college gist ycy: diuxde s'alme eyt m'cy, amen.[8]

This was the first master who held office from the foundation until 1382.

William White

This William headed a list of six chaplains in 1380, and by Michaelmas of 1382 had succeeded as master. In October of 1393 he obtained a papal dispensation to hold, together with his mastership, a benefice with a *curé*—within which he was not bound to reside.[9] It was White who investigated the Earl of Arundel's right of patronage. Again this master's brass survives in the chapel minus the inscription; however, it is known that he died on 20 February 1419, as borne out by the record taken by Tierney,[10] before the brass was vandalised:

> Hic jacet corpus humatum Dn' i Will', Whyte s'e'di Magr' i hui Coll' qui obiit XX die mensis Feb. A.D. MCCCCXIX . . . ac multa bona contulit huic collegio cujus anime propitietur Deus. Amen.

The words 'ac multa bona contulit huic collegio' demonstrate the great good he did for the college.

John Colmorde

Colmorde was presented to the mastership on 5 April 1421, 13 months after the death of White, his predecessor. The presentation was made by the king, because after such a lapse of time it reverted to the crown. He had already been a chaplain from 1406-1407.[11] He continued in the mastership until sometime before 1451.

Edward Poynings

Poynings is first recorded as master in 1451 in an indenture dated 28 April.[12] He was the son of Robert, Lord Poynings. He had a twin brother, Robert, who married Elizabeth, the only daughter of Sir William Paston, and as a result of this alliance a rather discreditable mention is given of the master in the famous Paston letters. The elder brother of this master, one Richard Poynings, married Eleanor, the widow of John, Earl of Arundel, thus making Earl William the stepson of Edward's brother. He died in office having obtained a prebendal stall at Chichester cathedral.

John Neal

John Neal was admitted as master on 19 March 1484. He is described in Bishop Story's register as a Master of Arts. His will is dated 10 March 1498.[13]

John Doget

Again Bishop Story's register supplied evidence. John Doget is referred to as Master of the College in 1499 and also a Doctor of Canon Law. As well as master he was treasurer of Chichester cathedral and rector of Eastbourne. His will is dated 4 March 1501.[14]

Henry Ediall

Henry Ediall was admitted to the mastership on 28 June 1501. He was also Archdeacon of Rochester and Provost of Wingham College, Suffolk, and rector of East Dereham, Norfolk. He died sometime before 1520.[15]

Edward Higgons

Edward Higgons was admitted to the mastership on 28 August 1520. He came from the family of Higgons of South Stoke and was described in the episcopal register as Doctor of Canon Law. The register of Oxford University (1500-1715) describes him as a law graduate in 1507, becoming a doctor in 1511. He was principal of Burnell's Inn, in the parish of St. Aldgates, London, and a king's chaplain. He also seems to have held a canonry in the Collegiate church of St. Stephen, Westminster, and a prebendal stall in Chichester Cathedral.[16]

Alan Percy

Alan Percy first appears in the collegiate rolls as master in 1539/40. He was the third son of Henry, Earl of Northumberland. The Percys had long held lands in Sussex, including Petworth. He was a prebendary of York cathedral and rector of St. Anne, Aldersgate. In 1615-18 he had been Master of St. John's College, Cambridge. He was also rector of St. Mary-at-Hill, London. His name with that of two chaplains appears on the college's deed of surrender of December 1544. He had apartments in the castle, and his name is still used to describe the vicinity of his lodgings. After the Dissolution he became rector of Storrington, and subsequently Eartham, where he presumably died in 1560.[17]

College Personnel taken from the Arundel Castle archives

Adam Ertham	1st master
Wm. White	2nd
John Colmorde	3rd
Ed. Poynings	4th
John Neal	5th
John Dogget	6th
Hy Ediall	7th
Ed. Higgon	8th
Alan Percy	9th

Rob. Adenat	sub-master, 1394/5
John Robroke	sub-master, 1407
Adam Soult	sub-master, 1430–6

John Mundy	acting sub-deacon, 1459/60
	chaplain, 1476/7
	sub-master, 1478 (–1500–?)

John Orley	bursar, 1499-1500
John Clerke	clerk to steward of the hospice, 1530-1
John Barber	steward of the hospice, 1440/1
John Pedlyn	1442/3
John Baker	steward of the hospice, 1440/1
Ric. Blome	instructor of choristers, 1459/60

| John Wyltshire | receiver, 1410-11 (A.C.A.4) |

Wm. Whyte	master
Esperaunce Blondel	deputy
John Shyrbone	cantor
Tho. Kyng	principal sacristan
Henry Bonsyre	other sacristan

| Richard Hendyman | 1419-20 (C.A.5) |

Wm. White	master
Adam Smyth	deputy
Tho. Kyng	principal sacristan
John Champion	principal chaplain to teach the boys 'song'

| Ric. Hendyman | 1420-21 (C.A.6) |

John Colmorde	master
Adam Smyth	deputy
Tho. King	principal sacristan
John Champyon	'schoolmaster for song'

| Richard Rowland | receptor, 1425-6 (C.A.7) |

| *John Colmorde* | master |

| John Pedelyn | collector, 1430/1 (C.A.8) |

| *John Colmorde* | master |

1436-7 (C.A.9)

John Colmorde	master
Hugo Bunne	
John Rake	chaplain
John Carter	deacon
John Champyon	sub-master and cantor
John Waldebef	clerk No. 1
John Colmorde	clerk No. 2
John Barbour	
Ric. Bussell	
John Seyte	
John Duffe	
John Pedlyn	master's servant
Henry Macheon	
Ric. Bussell	playing organ
Ric. Petron	principal sacrist

1458-59 (A.C.A.13)

Ed. Ponynges	master
Ric. Blome	clerk
John Wolball	deacon
John Dusse	sub-deacon
John Mundy	sub-deacon, organist
Richard Smyth	clock-keeper
John Grey	clerk
Wm. Coventre	chorister
John Walball	for his diligence about masses and antiphons
The Scolemaister	schoolmaster
Ric. Cleus	clerk

(Dorse 9-10 Henry VII) bursar's accnt. (C.A.18)

John Neale	master
John Munday	
J. Wepham	chaplain
J. Esshyng	,,
Tho. Dyar	,,
Ralf Sharp	,,
J. Colingtrow	,,
Rob. Farnedale	,,
Tho. Lenard	,,
Wm. Fairford	deacon
John Alenson	,,

Nic. Huichon	sub-deacon
Wm. Eliot	,,
Mich. Curson	clerk for 3 terms
Nich. Brelle	for 2 terms
Tho. Rosse	for 14 weeks
John Walsshman	12 weeks
John Stubbar	
John Frankelen	for 3 terms
Chris. Tompson	for 2
Wm. Cowper	chorister
Rob. Pinbridge	,,
John Peade	,,
John Parker	,,
Chris. Tomson	inducted for 2 terms etc.
Wm. Meriman	1st sacrist
Ralph Patte	sub-sacrist
John Wepham	late bursar
John Esshying	bursar
John Dogete	master, occ. 1499 (*Arundel College*)
	occ. 1501
	d. 1501

succeeded by *Hy. Edyall*

Henry Ediall	d. by 28 August 1520
Ed. Higgons	d. dec. 28 August 1520

EP 1/18/4

Visitation of the College of Arundel 13 July Anno predicto (1543)

Alan Percy	master
Thomas Wells	sub-master
Edward Lutwych	
William Lutwych	
William Bowdler	
John White	
John Parkyn	
George Elsden	
John Fygyn	
Thomas Blackwell	
Antony Byshop[18]	

John Wyseman	clerk
William Edwards	,,
William Goodweyne	,,
Peter Ansty	,,
Robert Wade	,,
William Lawson	,,
Thomas Foster	,,
Thomas Ryly	,,
John Gendon	acolite
John Alltrop	,,

Rectors of Arundel since 1380

(with right of presentation)

The Benedictine Priory Church of St. Nicholas had Priors who were also Rectors of Arundel from 1102 to 1380.

In 1380 the Priory being dissolved the rectorship passed to the master of the newly-established College of Secular Canons on the same site. The parish church retained the dedication to St. Nicholas.

The Masters of Arundel College

Adam Ertham	1380
William White	1382
John Colmorde	1421
Edward Poynings	1451
John Neal	1484
John Doget	1499
Henry Ediall	1501
Edward Higgons	1530
Alan Percy	1539[19]

The college ended with the dissolution of the religious houses in 1558—in the same year the old English hierarchy likewise came to an end.

Penal Times

(Arundel Catholics served from Slindon House, 1558–1748)

Missionary Priests

		(date of residence)
Anthony Bruning	..	1689
Henry Kempe ..	..	1698
William Lane ..	before 1738

Domestic Chaplains to the Duke of Norfolk at Arundel Castle

Charles Cordell	..	1748
Joseph Addis ..	..	1772
— Fishwick ..	..	1780
Philip Wyndham	..	1785*
Mark Tierney ..	..	1858*
John Butt ..	..	1858*

*Resident in Arundel College, serving the public oratory in the west wing.
(Re-establishment of English Catholic Hierarchy in 1850.)

*Rectors of the Parish Church of St. Philip (founded 1873), and
Domestic Chaplains to the Dukes of Norfolk*

(In 1965 becoming cathedral of Our Lady and St. Philip)

John Butt ..	..	..	1873	Edward Browne ..	..	1945
John Burke..	..	..	1885	David Cashman ..	..	1956
Archibald MacCall		..	1898	John Jeffries ..	..	1958
John Cuddon	..	..	1927	Christopher Aston	..	1967
Stanley Monnington		..	1937	John Grant ..	..	1972
Arthur Dudley	..	..	1939	Bernard Thom ..	..	1978

Chapter V

THE HOSPITAL OF THE HOLY TRINITY

RICHARD, the third Earl of Arundel, who died in 1376, had originally intended to found a hospice for the aged poor attached to his College of the Holy Trinity. However, like the college itself, this aim remained for his successor, the fourth earl to fulfil. Richard, the fourth earl, faithful to his father's wishes, set about instituting the intended hospice as soon as the collegiate building had been established. In March of 1395 he obtained the site (consisting of four messuages and two tofts) in Arundel, and conveyed the same to the master and community of the College of the Holy Trinity. This was to be held by them for the purpose of erecting an 'Almshouse' for the aged and inform poor.[1]

The site was a little way from the college on the edge of the town under the western wall of the castle. The ground was prepared and the foundations were laid and by the end of a year (1396) the building was standing. In shape, it much resembled the college, with a quadrangle containing chapel and refectory and all the necessary offices and the chambers of the almsmen. There was a cloister and the main entrance was by a gateway on the south-west corner. The statutes for the hospice were drawn up by Earl Richard, and stipulated the qualifications necessary for admission. The foundation was devised to care for 20 poor men, who were not married or widowers, and who as a result of poverty, age, or sickness, could no longer provide for their own sustenance. These 20 were to be taken from the surrounding areas, preference being given to the servants or tenants of the founder and his heirs. They were to be of good character and able to recite the *Pater Noster*, the *Ave Maria*, and the *Credo* in Latin.[2] The almsmen

29

were to be governed by a priest with the title of 'Master', who in turn was to be chosen by the founder or his heirs from among the most suitable members of the College of the Holy Trinity. If the college failed to supply a suitable candidate then he was to be chosen from among the other secular clergy. The master was to be both superior and chaplain, and was to be in continual residence in the hospital. In this way he could supervise the conduct of the inmates and ensure their comfort and well-being and by a fatherly concern protect their interests. He it was who decided admission to the hospital, received the oath of the almsmen upon reception, each in turn, and bound members to honour the statutes. The master had the authority to correct and even expel any member of the hospital to ensure obedience and the good ordering of the community.

To assist the master in his work a member of the community was to be elected by his fellows as prior. The duty of the prior was to superintend recreation and to ensure attendance in chapel, refectory and dormitory as the rule prescribed. The prior also supervised the conduct of the almsmen and none could leave the hospital without his permission or that of his delegate. Apart from master and prior a steward was to be appointed for the administration of the property, and at the end of each year he, with the master, had to produce a statement on the maintenance of what the hospital possessed. The community in turn provided auditors who examined the accounts. This done, an inventory of the foundation's possessions was appended to the annual report and deposited in the community's muniments.[3]

Apart from the three officers, four servants were to be appointed, one of these being a clerk who was to be the assistant of the master, while the others were to attend on the community. The daily routine of the hospital placed the spiritual care of the inmates first in priority. In summer they were bidden to rise at five of the clock, and in winter an hour later; before quitting their dormitories they were obliged to give themselves to prayer. This in turn would be followed by the celebration of Mass at which all who were capable were expected to attend. During the course of the day the almsmen would be assigned special tasks: work in the garden; weeding church paths; or assisting in the hospital, nursing the sick or supervising the distribution of clothing. All according to their strength or abilities found occupation, and those too infirm to do aught were commended to prayer and meditation.

At noon there was another summons to prayer; those who were more nimble climbed the hill to the collegiate chapel, while the remainder made their orisons in the dormitory. Midday prayer was followed by the main meal, and this in turn by recreation or the afternoon's activities. The day proceeded with evening prayer and supper, and at the hour of six a bell would strike (half-past six in summer) to signal attendance in the dormitory where final prayers would be offered and all retired for the night; only the master and the prior being excused this obligation.[4]

The almsmen dressed in long coarse brown woollen garments with cowls, not unlike a monastic habit. This uniform, together with shoes and socks, would each Christmas be presented to all the members of the hospital. At Easter there was a similar distribution of linen. If any member of the community fell sick they were to be nursed by their fellows, the hospital bearing any necessary expenses. In the case of leprosy the patient was to be withdrawn, presumably to the care of the nearby Leper Hospital of St. James,[5] but was to continue in receipt of a penny a day as the minimum standard amount allocated for his maintenance. If the unfortunate should sufficiently recover to return to the hospital he had to content himself as a subordinate.

The hospital accounts which remain start at Michaelmas of 1407. The possessions of the foundation at that time consisted of Sullington, Heen, Lychepole, 'Feld and Knell', and a tenement in Arundel. The total income derived from these was only £50 11s. ½d.[6] It must be remembered that the founder (Richard, fourth Earl of Arundel) had met with an untimely end at the hand of a peculiarly vindictive sovereign and his little foundation must have suffered accordingly. As witness to this the community numbered, with its master, a mere 15 souls in all. Earl Richard's son, Thomas, the fifth Earl, however, made good his father's pious intentions, and in his will, dated 10 October 1415, he ensured that property in

Birdham, Treyford, Northwood, Eartham, Ilesham, Tortington, Warningcamp, Kingston (near Lewes), and Bartholomews (Brighton?) was conveyed to the hospital. Thus by 1437 the annual income had risen to £101 13s. 10¼d. This figure, however, was not to be sustained, for by 1533 the rental was down to £89 5s. 2d., and in the year before the hospital was dissolved in 1545 the annual income had not risen above £93 18s. 6¾d.[7]

Chapter VI

THE FOUNDER

RICHARD FITZALAN, fourth Earl of Arundel, was son and heir to his father, the third earl, by his second wife, Eleanor Beaumont, daughter of the Duke of Lancaster. He was born in 1346 and was made a Knight of the Garter by the time he was thirty. This was the year he succeeded to the earldom, and the following year he was selected to bear the crown at Richard II's coronation.[1] Within that same year he was chosen as a member of the new council to supervise the government of the realm during the king's minority, and appointed admiral of the west and south. Early in his career he suffered an humiliating defeat with his uncle, the Duke of Lancaster, when, on an expedition against Bretagne, victory was snatched from him by his own negligence.[2] He apparently soon regained the confidence of his superiors, for when the young king came of age and the regency had ended, he was appointed head of the lay commissioners selected to look into the running of the royal exchequer. This was in 1380, the same year in which he founded the College of Arundel. The following year with Sir Michael de la Pole he was given charge of 'the counsel and government of the King's person'.[3] In 1383 he joined forces with an army despatched to drive back the Scots. In this he distinguished himself and subsequently was appointed admiral of the English fleet;[4] the fleet had been raised to defend the English coast against France (Scotland's ally). The French fleet, in fact, met a storm and was dispersed off the coast of Thanet, which so dispirited the Constable of France that the expedition was called off.

Upon his return Earl Richard became enmeshed in political intrigues which were to dog the rest of his career. The great lords had begun to plot the overthrow of the government to

which the earl lent his might. It is quite possible that pangs
of jealousy had driven him to this extreme, for the king had
surrounded himself with favourites on whom he had conferred
especial honours. Sir Michael de la Pole had become Earl of
Suffolk, and Robert de Vere (Earl of Oxford), Duke of Ireland.
At the king's summoning of parliament in October of 1383
he received the demand that he dismiss members of his council.
The king resisted, but after three months was compelled to
dismiss his favourites. Earl Richard thereupon received the
appointment to preside at the trial of one of them—the Earl
of Suffolk, who, being found guilty of some frivolity, was fined
and imprisoned. After this the great lords proposed a council
for the remedy of abuses in the government, headed by the
Duke of Gloucester and the Earl of Arundel. However, the
king at first would not countenance such a move, but with
pressure he finally agreed, and so transferred his power to the
confederate lords for a period of 12 months. Earl Richard was
now appointed Admiral of England and proceeded to win a
number of brilliant sea victories.[5]

The king's power was restored after the 12 months had
elapsed, but he was in an ill humour at the loss of his dignity,
and hostile towards the confederate lords, which the Earl of
Arundel's victories had done little to mitigate. Added to this
the king's favourites were determined on revenge. Meantime,
Earl Richard, somewhat in disgust, had retired from court life
to his castle at Ryegate, but within a few days men at arms were
despatched to arrest him. He escaped through the timely
warning of the Duke of Gloucester and joined him in raising an
army to oppose the king.

King Richard, learning that the army had reached Hackney,
became alarmed and issued a proclamation declaring the earl a
traitor and forbidding him aid.[6] Arundel and Gloucester had
now been joined by the Earls of Nottingham, Derby and Warwick. To reassure the king of their intentions they declared
that far from being treasonable they simply wished to punish
the 'traitors' who surrounded the throne. The king at last agreed
to meet them at Westminster on Sunday, 17 November 1387.
This done, the confederate lords pleaded their case against the
king's advisers, but avowed loyalty to his person. The king

treated them cordially and gave them his protection, and two days later he had the Earl of Arundel's innocence proclaimed. Meanwhile the Duke of Ireland had raised an army in the king's name against the confederate lords, and battle was eventually joined at Radcot Bridge. Ireland's force was vanquished and the victorious lords demanded an audience with the king; this was immediately granted, at which the terrified monarch was accused of conspiracy, and at once yielded to the lords' demands. The king's counsellors were arrested and eight were beheaded as traitors.

The confederate lords thus administered the realm for 12 months, at the end of which the king asserting his power dismissed them from office—Arundel losing command of the navy. Immediately the disconsolate earl requested permission to go abroad,[7] fearing the climate of the times, but returned shortly after and appeared reconciled with his enemies. Court life began to pall on him once again, and he retired, no doubt to the comparative calm of his castle at Arundel, where he could view the development of his College of Secular Canons.

On 12 June 1397 he was commanded to attend upon the king in private conference. No sooner had he arrived than he was straightway forcibly escorted to the Tower and thence to Carisbrooke Castle, on the Isle of Wight.[8] Arundel's confederates were likewise apprehended and all were accused of treason. On Friday, 21 September, Earl Richard was conducted to Westminster for his trial and there being found guilty of treason was led out to immediate execution on Tower Hill. His cheerful demeanour captivated the crowd, who afterwards followed his mortal remains to their burial at the church of the Austin Friars in Bread Street.[9]

Indeed, in mind of the late earl's pious works, not least the foundation of Arundel College, many accorded him the accolade of martyrdom, and went in pilgrimage to his tomb. Miracles were reported, and it was claimed that as a mark of Earl Richard's sanctity his head had been miraculously joined to his body. King Richard hearing these reports ordered the disinterment of the body one night, and this being done and no miraculous change being evident the tomb was destroyed and the earl's body hidden in obscurity beneath the church pavement. After King Richard's death the earl's son, the fifth of his line, erected a sumptuous tomb of marble to his father over the original place of burial.[10] Although fate dealt unkindly with Earl Richard he was revered by many as a man of piety and social conscience, as witnessed by his foundation of Arundel College and the Hospital of the Holy Trinity. In the cartulary of Tichfield Abbey there are documents dated in the year 1380,[11] when he commenced his great work at Arundel, which attest his desire to be admitted into the brotherhood of the Abbey and to have his share of the community's prayer and religious observance.

In his will, dated 1392, after reciting the nature and objects of the institution, which, he says, he has partially endowed, the earl adds:

> And for such part of the said endowment, as the master and chaplains shall not have obtained in full possession, at the time of my decease, I will that they and their successors continue to receive the annual rent, secured to them on my manors of Angmering, Wepham, Warningcamp, Southstoke, Tottington, Upmarden, and Peppering; and that, in discharge of all arrears of the same, my heirs and executors give and appropriate to them for ever such lands and churches as will fairly liquidate all demands. Moreover, considering that my late honoured father bequeathed to me, by will, certain vessels, jewels, and books, of which the greater part was to remain for ever attached to his intended chantry, in the chapel within the Castle, and that the said chantry is now, for reasons already recited, transferred to the parochial church, I desire that, for their better preservation, and for the greater merit of my father, these vessels, jewels, and books, with other ornaments for the chapel, which I have already given to the college, be and remain appurtenant thereto for ever, in the same manner as the other things which I have devised to the same purpose, and which I hereby order to be delivered to the community immediately after my death. I further desire, in particular, that the college be also put in possession of the other cloths and vestments for the chapel, and of the white silk vestments, both large and small, embroidered with M's, and given to me by my mother of Norfolk.[12]

PEDIGREES OF THE EARLS OF ARUNDEL OF THE HOUSE OF FITZ ALAN

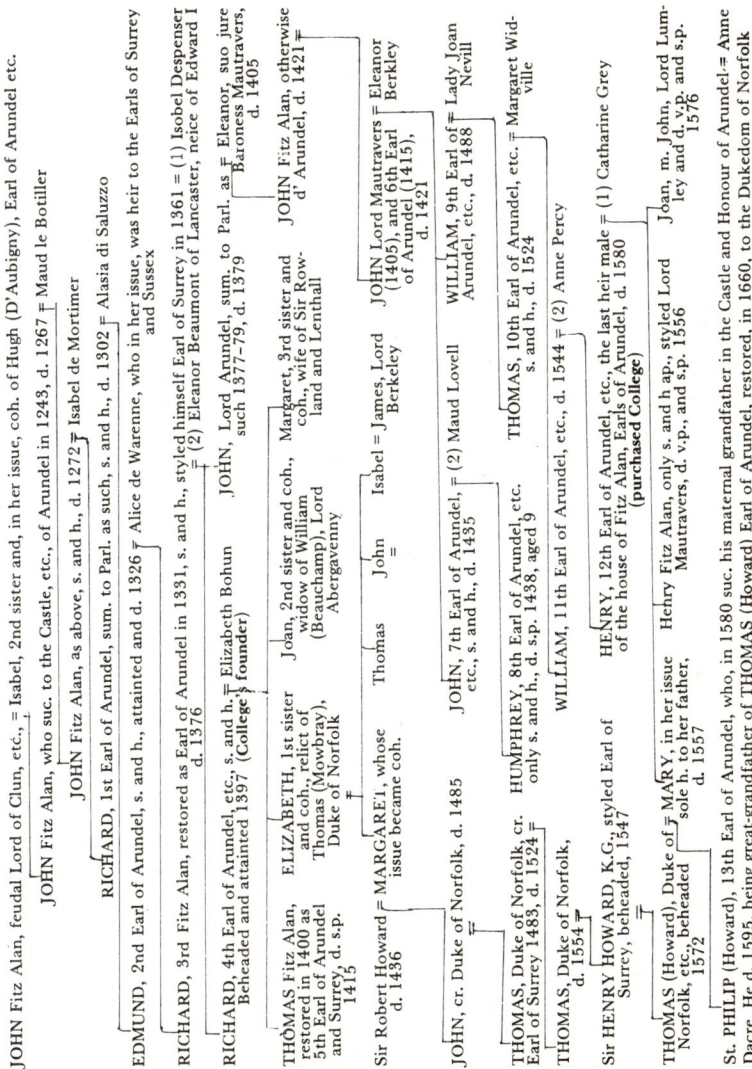

JOHN Fitz Alan, feudal Lord of Clun, etc., = Isabel, 2nd sister and, in her issue, coh. of Hugh (D'Aubigny), Earl of Arundel etc.

JOHN Fitz Alan, who suc. to the Castle, etc., of Arundel in 1243, d. 1267 = Maud le Botiller

JOHN Fitz Alan, as above, s. and h., d. 1272 = Isabel de Mortimer

RICHARD, 1st Earl of Arundel, sum. to Parl. as such, s. and h., d. 1302 = Alasia di Saluzzo

EDMUND, 2nd Earl of Arundel, s. and h., attainted and d. 1326 = Alice de Warenne, who in her issue, was heir to the Earls of Surrey and Sussex

RICHARD, 3rd Fitz Alan, restored as Earl of Arundel in 1331, s. and h., styled himself Earl of Surrey in 1361 = (1) Isobel Despenser
d. 1376 = (2) Eleanor Beaumont of Lancaster, neice of Edward I

RICHARD, 4th Earl of Arundel, etc., s. and h. = Elizabeth Bohun   JOHN, Lord Arundel, sum. to Parl. as = Eleanor, suo jure
Beheaded and attainted 1397 (College) founder)   such 1377–79, d. 1379   Baroness Mautravers,
d. 1405

JOHN Fitz Alan, otherwise
d' Arundel, d. 1421 =

THOMAS Fitz Alan,   ELIZABETH, 1st sister   Joan, 2nd sister and coh.,   Margaret, 3rd sister and
restored in 1400 as   and coh., relict of   widow of William   coh., wife of Sir Row-
5th Earl of Arundel   Thomas (Mowbray),   (Beauchamp), Lord   land and Lenthall
and Surrey, d. s.p.   Duke of Norfolk   Abergavenny
1415

JOHN Lord Mautravers = Eleanor
(1405), and 6th Earl   Berkley
of Arundel (1415),
d. 1421

Sir Robert Howard = MARGARET, whose   Thomas   John   Isabel = James, Lord
d. 1436   issue became coh.   =   Berkeley

WILLIAM, 9th Earl of = Lady Joan
Arundel, etc., d. 1488   Nevill

JOHN, cr. Duke of Norfolk, d. 1485   JOHN, 7th Earl of Arundel, = (2) Maud Lovell
etc., s. and h., d. 1435

THOMAS, 10th Earl of Arundel, etc., = Margaret Wid-
s. and h., d. 1524   ville

THOMAS, Duke of Norfolk, cr.   HUMPHREY, 8th Earl of Arundel, etc.
Earl of Surrey 1483, d. 1524 =   only s. and h., d. s.p. 1438, aged 9

THOMAS, Duke of Norfolk,   WILLIAM, 11th Earl of Arundel, etc., d. 1544 = (2) Anne Percy
d. 1554 =

Sir HENRY HOWARD, K.G., styled Earl of   HENRY, 12th Earl of Arundel, etc., the last heir male = (1) Catharine Grey
Surrey, beheaded, 1547   of the house of Fitz Alan, Earls of Arundel, d. 1580
(purchased College)

THOMAS (Howard), Duke of = MARY, in her issue   Henry Fitz Alan, only s. and h ap., styled Lord   Joan, m. John, Lord Lum-
Norfolk, etc., beheaded   sole h. to her father,   Mautravers, d. v.p., and s.p. 1556   ley and d. v.p. and s.p.
1572   d. 1557   1576

St. PHILIP (Howard), 13th Earl of Arundel, who, in 1580 suc. his maternal grandfather in the Castle and Honour of Arundel.= Anne
Dacre. He d. 1595, being great-grandfather of THOMAS (Howard) Earl of Arundel, restored, in 1660, to the Dukedom of Norfolk

*For numbering of earls see footnote 13

Chapter VII

DISSOLUTION

THE COLLEGE continued to flourish for one and a half centuries marked by no outstanding events. This must be seen as a result of the community's faithful compliance with their founder's wishes, giving an example of pious order and consistent virtue. There is no record extant among the episcopal visitations of any laxity in the functions of the college or any suspected licentiousness or lapse in moral behaviour. The only misdemeanours on record are a notable absence of four brethren from choir on one occasion and a few matters of internal discipline. The internal matters refer to the irregularity of the master's accounts and suspected neglect of the college building's repair.[1] Another matter concerned the absence of Edward Higgons, the master, during which William Pynor the sub-master had died. During this unprecedented situation the Precentor by the name of Cotes took possession of the keys and doled out stipends to the brethren from the college treasury. Cotes was reprimanded when the master returned. This took place during a visitation in 1524, and three years later another complaint was raised before the visiting bishop. Crockwell, the sub-master, complained of misbehaviour in choir; the culprits it was discovered were two clerks, one Hawkins, and one Higgins, who were in the habit of holding conversations during divine office ('communitor fabulanter in choro, tempore divinorum'). Hawkins was also accused of violently assaulting one of the stewards beneath the college precincts (ad percutiendum seneschallum, infra precincutum collegii').[2] These misdemeanours are, however, of small account.

The monies the founding earl had used to endow the college were drawn from the revenues of the dissolved priory, which income was to be increased by the founder and his successors.

From the college's total revenue after the deduction of all expenses £200 remained as income per annum.[3] As the value of money declined the college failed to increase the rents of tenants. The financial difficulties were brought to the attention of Thomas, the 10th earl, in 1496 who assigned further rents to the college amounting to £60 per annum. Notwithstanding this, by 1512 the brethren were unable to present four-tenths of their income, as levied from all benefices in the archdiocese of Canterbury, for the support of the war with France. Henry VIII had obtained this support with the consent of convocation, but the college brethren were forced to plead their poverty and petitioned to be relieved of this levy. In the event they were granted a special licence which exempted them from paying any of the said tax.[4] The whole endowment at this time only reached £168 0s. 7¾d., which was inadequate even for the ordinary expenses of college life.

Throughout the existence of the college the brethren had displayed unimpeachable conduct and had shown a model rectitude in keeping the rules and fulfilling their various duties. Also the paucity of their income must have ensured anything but an indulgent existence. However, King Henry's insatiable demands were such that after he had determined to dissolve all religious houses that were considered lax or luxurious, the others were not to remain inviolate for long, despite the small revenue they offered. Thus under the Acts of 1545 and of 1547 all colleges, free-chapels, hospitals and fraternities were to be suppressed. In spite of these measures the king, as late as 1541, bargained with the College of Arundel and granted some monastic land (already requisitioned) in return for the college's manor of Bury. The monastic land in question was Hayling Island, formerly owned by the Charter-house of Sheen; a parcel of land in Shipley, Sussex, formerly belonging to the Hospitaller Knights of St. John together with their principle commandery in Sussex, at Poling, with the lands, tenements, chapel, liberties, woods and other appur-tenances.[6] The possession of the Poling commandery is of particular interest in view of the later history of the college, when the Knights of St. John returned to Sussex to take up possession of the college buildings. (The college was to hold this property in perpetuity by the annual service of half a knight's fee and the payment of the annual rent of £6 14s. 10½d.[7] At first it would seem that the college was favoured in that while other religious foundations were being dissolved wholesale, it received further endowments. Despite these emoluments the college continued to become impoverished, which led Thomas, the 10th Earl of Arundel, to seek a royal licence to alienate additional sources of income to the college. On 15 November 1496 this was granted, but the embursement was not to exceed £60 per annum.[8])

In 1535 one Richard Layton, visiting religious houses on behalf of the crown, wrote a letter to Thomas Cromwell dated 24 September, in which he stated his intention to visit Arundel College.[9] Along with the other colleges Arundel survived after the dissolution of the houses of the religious orders, but by the Acts of 1545 and 1547 most of the colleges came to an end, including Arundel. On 28 September 1542 William Fitzalan, 11th Earl of Arundel, had written to King Henry informing him of the college's existence, as founded by his ancestor the 4th earl, and begged the king's consent to him acquiring the college. To this end he promised the king 1,000 marks if he agreed.[10] The king's reply is not recorded, but in January 1544 Lord Matravers succeeded his father as the 12th Earl of Arundel and on 12 September of that year the college with all its possessions was surrendered to the Crown. This was technically illegal as it was 11 months before the passage of the Act through parliament to legalise the suppression![11] The deed of surrender was duly drawn up and signed by the last master of the college, Alan Percy (son of the Earl of Northumberland, and maternal uncle of the Earl of Arundel) and two of the brethren, John and Robert Fygnt. The deed relates that 'the said maters (*sic*), with the chaplains, or fellows, of the College of the Holy Trinity, at Arundel, after serious deliberation, did, unanimously, and of their own accord, in consideration of the many weighty and conscientious reasons specially moving them thereto, willingly, freely, and without reserve, for themselves and their successors, assign the said College, with the whole property and possession of the same, and all right, title and inheritance thereto, to the king and his heirs for ever.[12]

The college was surrendered to the royal commissioner, a Dr. Richard Rede. On 23 December the king granted to the 12th Earl of Arundel the site of the college and all its possessions, previously surrendered, for the consideration of 1,000 marks to be paid into the royal exchequer, and an annual rent of £16 16s. ¾d. Thus the earl regained possession of the college for himself and his heirs—including 'the site, lordships, manors, lands, tenements, and other hereditaments of the said College and chantry of the Holy Trinity, at Arundel'.[13] This was to be held for the tenth part of a knight's fee for ever. (This is of particular importance, for in 1879 the ownership of the college chapel was contested—see Appendix III: Duke of Norfolk v. Arbuthnot.)

The melancholy work of destruction was subsequently unleashed upon the empty college buildings, and all save the chapel and the master's residence and the kitchen wing were demolished.

Chapter VIII

THE CIVIL WAR AND LATER TIMES

THE COLLEGE thus left in ruins became a quarry for the needs of other buildings. Apart from this and general decay it was again slighted by the parliamentary forces in the 17th century.

On 22 August 1642 King Charles I raised his standard at Nottingham and England was plunged into civil war. Many of the great houses favoured the king's cause and held out against protracted siege by the parliamentary forces. Arundel was to be the scene of considerable military activity during these warlike engagements, and the old college, despite its location outside the castle walls, was to prove of strategic importance.

The parliamentary high command appointed Sir William Waller to take charge of its forces south of the Thames. Fresh from his capture of Winchester, he arrived in December 1642 at the head of an army within the borders of Sussex. The parliamentary troops were on their way to lay siege to Chichester, but six miles out the castle of Arundel lay across their route. Sir William Waller, in commanding the parliamentary army, gave orders that the castle should be taken. The castle garrison was soon surprised and quickly overpowered, the parliamentary troops having blown in the main gate with a pétard, and a hundred of the king's horses and men captured, including Sir Richard Teachford and his son, and one Captain Goulding. These, plus other notable prisoners, were escorted to prison at the command of parliament.

At this time Thomas, 14th Earl of Arundel, was settled abroad, the previous year having escorted Charles I's daughter, Mary, to Holland, where she was to become the wife of William of Orange. The Earl was never to return to England, but settled in Padua in 1644 where he died on 4 October two years later. Meanwhile Arundel without its earl suffered divided loyalties, and it seems that the ease with which the parliamentary forces took Arundel Castle was partly facilitated by the collusion of the local burgesses.[1] This situation obtained until 9 December 1643, when the castle was besieged by a royalist army under Lord Hopton. The assault was led by Sir Edward Ford, and Sir Edward Bishop, who overpowered the garrison, being short of victuals and ammunition and unused to war, soon capitulated.[2]

Parliament re-acted sharply to this royalist victory and appointed John Baker of Mayfield as High Sheriff of Sussex, and directed that a relief force be despatched with all expedition.

By 19 December 1643 Sir William Waller had returned and was camped 'on a heath within a mile of the town'.[3] Lord Hopton had placed Sir Edward Ford in command of the castle garrison, consisting of 200 men and many good officers. The parliamentary army commenced the attack on the town about 21 December, driving many townspeople to seek refuge in the old church of St. Nicholas. These were subsequently smoked out, not without some damage to the college precincts, and the church narrowly escaped destruction by burning.

The services in the college chapel had long since ceased, and during the siege Waller's men had damaged the chapel walls, mutilated tomb figures and altar stones and destroyed much of the stained glass. Not only had Waller's troopers used the chapel as a stable for their horses, but also an artillery-piece had been mounted on the roof to afford a closer range for the bombardment of the castle keep, and the hospital of the Holy Trinity was left a ruin.

The conclusion of the siege saw the royalist garrison surrender on 6 January 1644 under the terms stipulated by Sir William Waller. For nearly one hundred and fifty years after these events the ruined college and chapel remained in a dilapidated state. In a manuscript survey of 1702 the situation was described as follows:

The chancells at Arundell lye very indecently. It rains into the great chancell, and the roof thereof is, some of it, fallen down, and the rest will quickly follow if not repaired and kept dry. 'Tis a thousand pityes, being the finest thing, one of them, in that kind, I ever saw.[4]

★ PEDIGREE OF THE FITZALAN AND HOWARD FAMILIES ★

ALBINI

WILLIAM de ALBINI, 1st Earl of Arundel = ADELIZA of Louvain, widow of Henry I
(d 1176)

WILLIAM, 2nd Earl of Arundel (d. 1193) = MAUD de St. HILAIRE du HARCOUET

WILLIAM, 3rd Earl of Arundel (d. 1221) = MABEL Le MESCHIN

WILLIAM, 4th Earl of Arundel (d. 1224) — HUGH, 5th Earl of Arundel (d. 1243) — ISABEL = JOHN FITZALAN, Lord of Clun and Oswestry

JOHN FITZALAN of Arundel = MAUD Le BOTILLER
(d. 1267)

FITZALAN

JOHN FITZALAN of Arundel = ISABEL de MORTIMER
(d. 1272)

RICHARD FITZALAN 1st Earl of Arundel (d. 1302) = ALICE of Saluzzo

EDMUND, 2nd Earl of Arundel (d. 1326) = ALICE de WARENNE

RICHARD 3rd Earl of Arundel (d. 1376) = (2) ELEANOR of Lancaster
niece of Edward I

RICHARD = ELIZABETH BOHUN — JOHN Lord Arundel (drowned 1379) = ELEANOR MALTRAVERS
4th Earl of Arundel
(beheaded 1397)

JOHN FITZALAN (or Arundel) = ELIZABETH DESPENCER
(d. 1390)

THOMAS 5th Earl of Arundel (d. 1415) — ELIZABETH = (2) THOMAS, MOWBRAY Duke of Norfolk (opposite †)

JOHN 6th Earl of Arundel (d. 1421) = ELEANOR BERKELEY

JOHN 7th Earl of Arundel (d. 1435) = (2) MAUD LOVELL — WILLIAM 9th Earl of Arundel (d. 1487) = LADY JOAN NEVILL

HUMPHREY 8th Earl of Arundel (d 1438, aged 9)

THOMAS 10th Earl of Arundel (d 1524) = MARGARET WIDVILE

WILLIAM, 11th Earl of Arundel (d. 1544) = (2) ANNE PERCY

HENRY 12th Earl of Arundel (d 1580) = (1) CATHARINE GREY

LADY MARY FITZALAN (1) = THOMAS HOWARD 4th Duke of Norfolk*
(d. 1557)   (beheaded 1572)

HOWARD

EDWARD I King of England = (2) MARGARET of Valois
1272-1307

THOMAS of Brotherton = (1) ALICE de HALES
Earl of Norfolk* (d. 1338)

MARGARET, Duchess of Norfolk (d. 1399)

ELIZABETH SEGRAVE — JOHN, 4th Lord Mowbray (d. 1368) = (1) JOHN 4th Lord Segrave

THOMAS MOWBRAY 1st Duke of Norfolk* † (d. 1399) = (2) ELIZABETH FITZALAN (opposite)

LADY MARGARET MOWBRAY = SIR ROBERT HOWARD

JOHN HOWARD 1st Duke of Norfolk* (k. 1485) = (1) CATHERINE de MOLEYNS

THOMAS 2nd Duke of Norfolk* (d. 1524) = (1) ELIZABETH TILNEY

THOMAS, 3rd Duke of Norfolk* (d. 1554) = (2) LADY ELIZABETH STAFFORD

HENRY Earl of Surrey = LADY FRANCES VERE
(beheaded 1547)

★ indicates Marshal or Earl Marshal of England

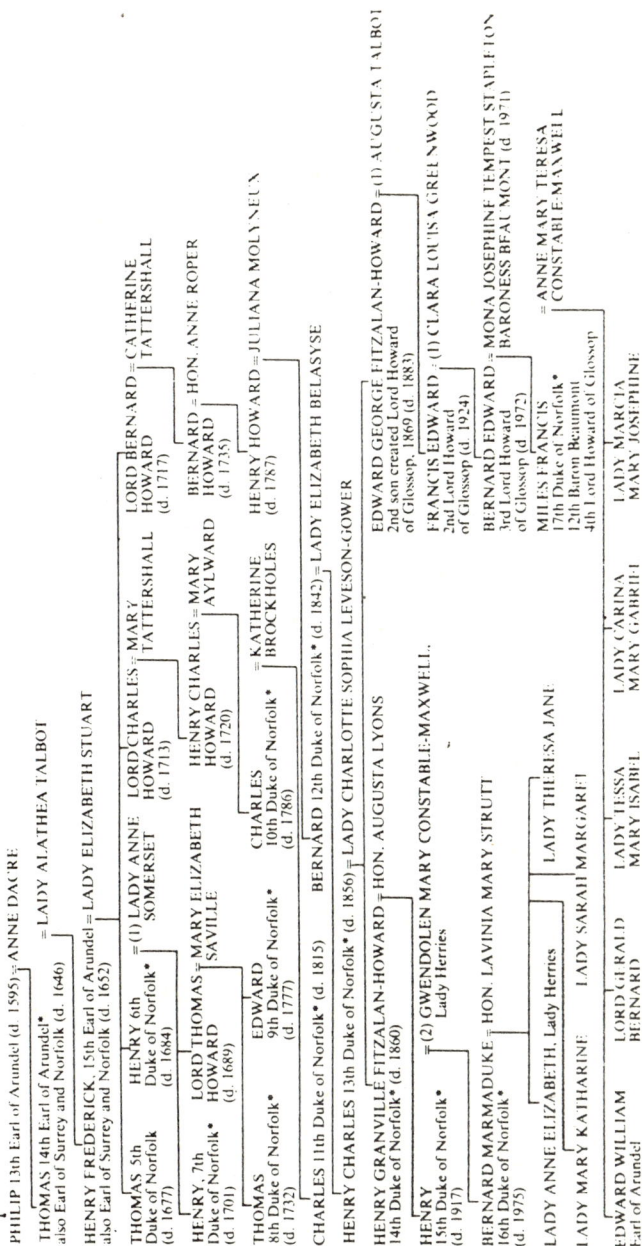

PHILIP 13th Earl of Arundel (d. 1595) = ANNE DACRE

THOMAS 14th Earl of Arundel* = LADY ALATHEA TALBOT
also Earl of Surrey and Norfolk (d. 1646)

HENRY FREDERICK, 15th Earl of Arundel = LADY ELIZABETH STUART
also Earl of Surrey and Norfolk (d. 1652)

THOMAS 5th Duke of Norfolk (d. 1677)

HENRY 6th Duke of Norfolk* (d. 1684) = (1) LADY ANNE SOMERSET

LORD CHARLES HOWARD (d. 1713) = MARY TATTERSHALL

HENRY CHARLES HOWARD (d. 1720) = MARY AYLWARD

LORD BERNARD HOWARD (d. 1717) = CATHERINE TATTERSHALL

BERNARD HOWARD (d. 1735) = HON. ANNE ROPER

HENRY HOWARD (d. 1787) = JULIANA MOLYNEUX

LORD THOMAS HOWARD (d. 1689) = MARY ELIZABETH SAVILLE

EDWARD 9th Duke of Norfolk* (d. 1777)

THOMAS 8th Duke of Norfolk* (d. 1732)

CHARLES 10th Duke of Norfolk* (d. 1786) = KATHERINE BROCKHOLES

CHARLES 11th Duke of Norfolk* (d. 1815)

BERNARD 12th Duke of Norfolk* (d. 1842) = LADY ELIZABETH BELASYSE

HENRY CHARLES 13th Duke of Norfolk* (d. 1856) = LADY CHARLOTTE SOPHIA LEVESON-GOWER

HENRY GRANVILLE FITZALAN-HOWARD 14th Duke of Norfolk* (d. 1860) = HON. AUGUSTA LYONS

EDWARD GEORGE FITZALAN-HOWARD 2nd son created Lord Howard of Glossop, 1869 (d. 1883) = (1) AUGUSTA TALBOT

FRANCIS EDWARD 2nd Lord Howard of Glossop (d. 1924) = (1) CLARA LOUISA GREENWOOD

BERNARD EDWARD 3rd Lord Howard of Glossop (d. 1972) = MONA JOSEPHINE TEMPEST STAPLETON BARONESS BEAUMONT (d. 1971)

MILES FRANCIS 17th Duke of Norfolk* 12th Baron Beaumont 4th Lord Howard of Glossop = ANNE MARY TERESA CONSTABLE-MAXWELL

LADY MARCIA MARY JOSEPHINE

HENRY 15th Duke of Norfolk* (d. 1917) = (2) GWENDOLEN MARY CONSTABLE-MAXWELL. Lady Herries

BERNARD MARMADUKE 16th Duke of Norfolk* (d. 1975) = HON. LAVINIA MARY STRUTT

LADY ANNE ELIZABETH, Lady Herries

LADY MARY KATHARINE

LADY THERESA JANE

LADY SARAH MARGARET

EDWARD WILLIAM Earl of Arundel

LORD GERALD BERNARD

LADY TESSA MARY ISABEL

LADY CARINA MARY GABRIEL

In 1782 Charles, 10th Duke of Norfolk (and 21st Earl of Arundel) ordered the old roof of the college chapel to be dismantled, including the parapets of the walls. The roof was stripped of its lead and with ruthless expedition the workmen employed for the task sawed through the heavy oak beams of the roof and allowed them to fall on the chapel below. Thus a magnificent medieval carved wooden ceiling was demolished and the great oak beams supporting the roof were allowed to crash down —crushing stalls, tombs, and even breaking the vaults beneath.

> As the immense timbers from above were torn from the walls, or cut from their supporters, they were suffered to fall, at random, on whatever might chance to lie beneath. Beam after beam was thus plunged from the extreme height of the chapel; the stalls were crushed, the tombs shattered, and the floor itself, which is laid over the vaults, was, in many instances, broken and forced in. A modern slated covering, without parapets, was now substituted for the ancient roof; and the conversion of the chapel into a temporary workshop a few years later, by enabling the workmen to purloin the brass ornaments that still remained, completed the desolation of the edifice.[5]

Although reduced to the status of a workshop with a mean slate roof the chapel continued to be used as a place of interment for members of the Howard family as the heirs to the Fitzalans. In 1847 the great vault under the high altar was constructed for future interments, the vault in the Lady Chapel having been used until that time.

In 1879 the Anglican vicar of Arundel, the Rev. George Arbuthnot, claimed the old college chapel (known as the Fitzalan Chapel) as the chancel of the parish church. Architecturally his assertion was correct, but as regards the chapel's separate status, this he failed to recognise (see Appendix III: Duke of Norfolk v. Arbuthnot). With a view to testing his right he proceeded to break through the intervening wall, which had been built by the 15th Duke of Norfolk on the east side of the 14th-century iron grille, which divides the chapel from the parish church. The case was brought before the Court of Common Pleas on 17 March 1879 and heard by Lord Justice Coleridge. When judgement was given on 17 May 1879 the case of 'the Duke of Norfolk versus the Rev. G. Arbuthnot' was established in the duke's favour, to the effect that the chapel was proved to be the private property of the Dukes of Norfolk, and was not part of the parish church.

Chapter IX

A NEW FOUNDATION

AFTER THE BOMBARDMENT of Arundel Castle during the Civil War it lay uninhabitable for nearly three centuries. The old college of the Holy Trinity lay in ruins, its chapel desecrated, and thus it all remained until Thomas, 8th Duke of Norfolk initiated some repair. This duke died in 1732 and his work of restoration was not to be continued until Charles, 11th duke succeeded, and introduced a fanciful style of Gothic to the castle, but caused the college chapel to be unroofed and made over as a carpentry shop! Between the years 1837 and 1844 the 12th and 13th dukes (23rd and 24th Earls of Arundel) made a concerted effort at the restoration of the college chapel. The 14th duke continued the restoration and built the mausoleum on the south side of the chapel (containing the tombs of himself and his wife). The 15th duke put in the fine east window in memory of his first wife, and restored the vaulted wooden ceiling complete with some of the original medieval roof bosses that a Captain William Kemp had discovered in an outhouse at Poling; thus by 1866 the chapel was well on the way to restoration.

The rest of the college buildings which survived consisted largely of the master's residence and kitchen wing; however, on the external side of the quadrangle the one wall remained entire. It was the 11th duke who took to restoring what was left of the college itself and set about repairing the existing buildings with the intention of providing a public oratory for the local Catholic population and his own family.[1] He chose the west end of the existing building for this purpose, converting the eastern part into accommodation for his chaplain 'Mr.'[2] Philip Wyndham, who served from 1785 to 1825.

47

Wyndham was succeeded by the famous antiquarian and his-
torian, 'Mr.' Mark Aloysius Tierney, who served as chaplain
to the oratory from 1825 to 1862: 'Mr.' John Butt (later
Bishop Butt) was appointed assistant in 1858 and succeeded
to the chaplaincy in 1862. All these clergy resided in the same
apartments in the east end of the college.

The section of the building used for the oratory is today
transformed into a theatre. It was some 42ft. long by 20ft.
wide until being lengthened by about 20ft. in 1865, and amply
accommodated the congregation, the duke and his family.
The oratory possessed a gallery (which can still be seen), a
classical altar with a picture of the adoration of the shepherds
(since returned to the castle), plain wooden altar rails and
benches divided by a central gangway. The retable of the altar
(upper portion), the tabernacle and the crucifix were all of
gilt bronze in the French renaissance style. This was made in
1730 and is now to be seen on the Lady Altar[3] in Arundel
Cathedral. At first Mass was only said in the oratory on Sundays
and holy days. During the week the altar would be encased
in wash leather, and in these early days of the Catholic mission
it is said that an aged caretaker amassed considerable wealth
by showing visitors what he described as the 'gold altar'.[4]

The old kitchen wing, contiguous with the chapel, was the
duke's agent's residence for a number of years. Then the 14th
Duke turned part of the college into a convent for Carmelite
nuns, and in 1861, a year after his death, these nuns were
succeeded by Sisters of the Servite Order. The Sisters came by
arrangement with the 14th Duke, made shortly before his
death.[5] This convent was known as St. Wilfred's, after the
apostle of West Sussex. Subsequently a laundry was established
in the convent for the requirements of the castle and oratory
(and later the new parish church of St. Philip), and a certain
number of girls were employed, being also trained for domestic
service.[6] The Sisters also ran a small school within the college,
which from about this time became known as 'The Priory'.

The old college building must have become a busy place with
convent, infant school, and the resident clergy—and thus it
continued until the establishment of Arundel as a Catholic
parish (as opposed to a mission) and the opening of the parish

church of St. Philip Neri on 1 July 1873. This saw the fulfilment of the ambition of Henry, the 15th duke, and thus John
Butt was withdrawn from the college and installed as first
rector of the church in a fine new Gothic rectory. This church
became a cathedral of the new diocese of Arundel and Brighton
in 1965 and was re-dedicated to our Lady and St. Philip
Howard in 1973.[7]

Meanwhile by 1960 the Servite Sisters had closed their school
and moved out of the old college buildings, having occupied
them for nearly one hundred years. The buildings were not
vacant for long, and from 1960 to 1974 'Arundel Priory', as
it has come to be known, was used as a children's home run
by a Mr. St. John Foti. The lease for this occupation having
run out by 1974 the family of the 16th duke had decided to use
the building as a home for the elderly. At the same time the
Chancellor of the Sovereign and Military Order of Malta was
looking for an historic building to turn into almshouses for the
elderly. This idea the Order had already pioneered and subsequently becoming acquainted with the Norfolk family's
wishes offered their services. As a result for a peppercorn rent
the old college was leased to the Order for the charitable assistance of the elderly, and the old college, which once received
the dissolved estates of the Order of St. John in the 16th
century, in the 19th century saw the same Order return as the
new tenants of the college.

Chapter X

THE ORDER OF ST. JOHN AND ARUNDEL COLLEGE

THE ORDER OF THE HOSPITAL of St. John of Jerusalem was founded by Master Gerard sometime towards the end of the 11th century. To this day there can still be seen in the Greek quarter of the old city of Jerusalem an old church dedicated to St. John the Baptist, from whence the order took its name; the site of the first hospital still has substantial remains, restored by Kaiser Wilhelm II of Germany, and which today serves as a hospice for Lutheran Christians. The Order anticipated by many centuries all other organisations dedicated to the care of the poor and the sick in its care for the poor and sick pilgrims in the Holy Land. With the increasing danger that unarmed pilgrims were often faced with, the Order raised a force of knights for their protection which soon developed into a regular army. Thus the Order came to be divided between the 'military' brethren and the 'infirmarian' brethren; among the latter were included the 'brother chaplains' who were responsible for the spiritual needs of each hospital or commandery (as the small serving detachments were called). The brethren took the three vows of poverty, chastity and obedience, and the military arm thus produced the phenomenon of soldier monks.

Raymund de Puy succeeded to the mastership in 1120 and with the advent of the Crusades the order spread through Europe. In England a headquarters was set up at Clerkenwell in London (Knightsbridge and St. John's Wood both took their name from the Order); each country had its own association or 'langue', and each association was divided up into districts or 'bailiwicks'. It is interesting to note that the London house was erected only eight[1] years after the Order's foundation

50

and with the advancing wealth and importance of the brethren the Grand Prior of England soon became the senior lay baron and took his seat in the House of Lords, as the 'Lord of St. John's'. Then in 1309 on a set of trumped-up charges the younger and rival Order of Knight Templars was suppressed and their property throughout Christendom was made over to the Order of St. John. In the county of Sussex the knights of St. John thus added to their possessions property at Shipley, Chichester, Saddlescombe, Cokeham in Sompting, and Compton.[2] Besides these the Order already possessed lands at Pococks, near Eastbourne, and at Midhurst. All this came under the Bailiwick of Poling which is believed to have been allotted to the knights by John FitzAlan of Arundel sometime after 1244.[3]

In 1341 Pococks in the manor of Ocklynge was confiscated by the crown on the pretext that the prior of the Order was not providing a chaplain for the commandery so that Mass could be said and alms distributed to the poor twice a week. Upon investigation it was discovered that the local commander, Brother (or Fra. as they are more traditionally called) Robert de Criel was under no such obligation, and moreover he himself had voluntarily distributed alms to those in need.[4]

The Poling commandery was endowed with lands from a number of parishes within the proximity of Arundel. These included Combe, Offham, Up Marden and Rumboldwyke. By 1338 the Combe and Offham lands were producing an annual revenue of £13 17s. 3d. for the commander at Poling. This added to other farms and lands made up a yearly income of £78 11s. 3d., which included alms collected in the neighbourhood. The annual running expenditure of the commandery was £34, leaving £44 11s. 3d. for the benefit of the Order, which would include the maintenance of the Poling commandery. The brethren at Poling in 1338 consisted of Peter atte Nasshe, knight preceptor, a fellow knight, Clement de Donewico, a chaplain, a steward or 'claviger', a cook, two attendants of the preceptor, and two clerks employed to collect alms ('confaria'). One of these clerks had lodgings in the commandery while the other probably had a roving commission. Over and above these nine brethren in residence and the travelling fundraiser there would also have been those employed in the herb garden, orchard, brewhouse, dairy farm, and various other types of agricultural labour.[5]

In 1381[6] the hundred and manor of Poling was settled on the newly-established College of Arundel by Earl Richard, the founder, but from then on the records of the Poling commandery are scant and little can be said of the brethren until the dissolution of the religious houses. In 1541, five years after the suppression of the lesser house, the Poling commandery together with all the Order's properties in England were dissolved and forfeited to the crown. By strange coincidence the Poling house and lands were made over to the college at Arundel, but not for long, for in 1546 the college itself was dissolved.

In the little church at Poling once served by the brethren of St. John there are to be seen some fine medieval roof bosses that once decorated the ceiling of the Fitzalan chapel (the chapel of Arundel College). The bosses are about 10in. or 11in. in diameter and date from the founding of the college in 1380. When in 1782 the 10th Duke of Norfolk had ordered the destruction of the chapel roof the bosses found their way into his possession. The 12th Duke in his turn presented them in about 1830 to the church at Poling, which was then undergoing restoration.[7] Only comparatively few of them were used, for by the early 19th century a Captain William Kemp of Lyminster House discovered the remainder in an old outhouse at Poling and promptly made them over to Henry, the 15th Duke, who used them for the restoration of the Fitzalan chapel ceiling.[8]

The Order of St. John, or the Sovereign, Military and Hospitaller Order of St. John of Jerusalem, Rhodes and Malta, to give it its full title, although no longer represented in England after the Reformation, continued to appoint titular priors to the one-time Grand Priory of England. Then, towards the end of the 19th century, the English association was eventually restored on the initiative of some French knights and has since continued to flourish. Some Englishmen from about 1831 onwards had hoped to form a Protestant branch of the Order, and acquired what remained of the original Order's headquarters at Clerkenwell (consisting largely of an old gateway), but were turned down by the masters in Rome. Thus they decided to go it alone and continued in an unofficial capacity until 1888, when they became formally constituted and given royal approbation, under the title of the Venerable Order of St. John. Since that time they have established the St. John's Ambulance Brigade and have since built an ophthalmic hospital in Jerusalem. The Parent Order also re-established a hospital at St. John's Wood, and the two Orders now enjoy mutual respect and co-operation in their care for the sick; as witness to this the old Arundel College (Priory) is now run as a home for the elderly poor by the Order of Malta Homes Trust, a joint venture with the Venerable Order of St. John and the Sovereign Order.

Chapter XI

THE CHAPEL OF THE HOLY TRINITY, OUR LADY AND ALL THE SAINTS AND THOSE BURIED THERE

THE CHAPEL consists of a single nave attached to the eastern end of the old parish church, measuring 82ft. 6in. in length, 28ft. in breadth, and 35ft. 6in. to the top of the walls. At the eastern end there is an exquisite plain mullioned window of seven lights, with much rich tracery in the upper part, and four smaller ones of like workmanship on the south side. On the north there is one similar to the latter, and three smaller ones. The original high altar, still entire, has a large altar stone of Purbeck marble and is placed against a screen of masonry, behind the private oratory of the masters of the old college.

Adjoining the chapel on the north side is the Lady Chapel, which was part of the original foundation, though completed at a later date. It is 54ft. 6in. long 26ft. wide, and is lighted by three northern windows, obtusely pointed; each with simple mullions and four principal lights, filled in the upper part with small pointed arches and ornamental designs, above which are canopies embellished with mouldings and crockets. The original altar and altar stone of Petworth marble are all in position, as is the niche around Our Lady's image. Here, according to the founder's statutes, a solemn Mass was to be sung daily, and later an additional Mass was introduced by Eleanor, Countess of Arundel, wife of John Fitzalan (d. 1421), 6th earl, in whose will (1455) the executors were ordered to spend 2,000 marks in establishing a chantry in this chapel to exist for a term of 26 years from her death, during which time a daily Mass was to be celebrated for the repose of her own and her husband's souls (which expired, of course, before the dissolution).

This chapel was founded ostensibly as a living memorial to the Fitzalan family; it is the most perfect tomb-house in England. The tombs, however, are intended as a reminder of mortality—of the implications of sins committed through human frailty, of the doctrine of expiation by prayer and good deeds, offered vicariously towards the redemption of the souls in purgatory. A chantry as such was endowed for the saying of Masses towards this end. As a chantry college one of the functions of the secular canons of this foundation was, in addition to the service of the parish church, the offering of prayers and Masses for the repose of the souls of the founders and their descendants.

Richard, 4th Earl of Arundel, in carrying out his intention to complete the college of the Holy Trinity and its chapel, was but complying with the intentions of his father. He alone was responsible for its location, outside the castle walls, thus affording some protection against French coastal raiders who might attack the castle. This earl (as previously stated) was beheaded by King Richard II and buried in the church of the Augustine Friars in Bread Street, London. Thus the monuments to the Fitzalan family in the college chapel begin with Thomas, 5th Earl of Arundel, and son of the founder. He was born in 1381 when King Richard II was 13 years old and in the second year of his reign. This Thomas died in 1415 at the age of 34 and was the first Fitzalan to be buried in what has now come to be called the Fitzalan Chapel. The third earl, Thomas's grandfather, died an enormously wealthy man, having succeeded not only to the estates of the earldom of Arundel but also the immense possessions of the earldom of Surrey. He left 90,359 marks 'in bags' in one of the towers of Arundel Castle and in the hands of certain receivers. The total amount of his fortunes, 108,295 marks, in terms of modern currency would be something of the order of £400,000,000— to satisfy the inland revenue.[1] Earl Thomas succeeded not only to all this through his father, but also to an illustrious tradition on the field of battle, his grandfather having been an all-victorious Admiral-in-Chief of the King's Fleet, and valiant commander of the Second Division at the Battle of Crécy (1346).

By the time Earl Thomas was three his father became involved in a dangerous form of enterprise. King Richard was in his twentieth year, and under the influence of worthless favourites. Richard Fitzalan was moved to join the Duke of Gloucester and press for the appointment of a commission to regulate the royal household and the kingdom. He succeeded, and later, as one of the Lords Appellant, he was instrumental in bringing about the Battle and victory of Radcot Bridge and the fall of the Court Party. Two years later, by which time our Earl Thomas was in his sixth year, King Richard II had taken the government into his own hands once more, and, apparently, for the next eight years ruled well. He made a reconciliation with the Lords Appellant, and in 1389 his uncle, the influential and powerful John of Gaunt, who three years previously had left the country for Spain, returned to England. In 1394 a special pardon for all his political offences was accorded to the Earl Richard, who then forsook public life and retired to Arundel, where he devoted himself to the building of the Maison Dieu (the Hospice of the Holy Trinity) according to his father's wish. The son, Earl Thomas, was now in his thirteenth year, and, by the time he was 15 (1396), the building of the Maison Dieu was finished. In 1397, within a few months of its completion, his father had been treacherously seized by the king and, on a trumped-up charge for offences pardoned years before, was tried, condemned to death, and led to immediate execution. After his execution his estates were alienated and given to John, Duke of Exeter.

Such, briefly, is the indication of the scene of Earl Thomas's boyhood and youth. He was now in his sixteenth year, his father vilely done to death, his belongings lost, his inheritance confiscated, himself committed to prison. Small wonder if his sympathies attached themselves to the cause of Henry, son of John of Gaunt, and the rival to the king.

Earl Thomas's connection with the Court of Portugal was that of second cousin to the queen. Beatrix, whom he subsequently married, was the natural daughter of the king of that country by Agnes Perez.

From Thomas's association with the cause of Henry, son of John of Gaunt, arose another connection, his identification with the Collar of SS[2] shown on his effigy on the central tomb in the Fitzalan Chapel. This Collar of SS, it is considered, was the secret sign of those who favoured the cause of John of Gaunt and his son Henry, and who were patiently awaiting their opportunity. After his father's execution, Earl Thomas was placed under arrest. He was then committed to close confinement in the Castle of Reigate under the Duke of Exeter; but, escaping to France, he joined his uncle, the exiled Archbishop of Canterbury. On 4 July 1399, in his eighteenth year, he landed in England with Henry, whose father, John of Gaunt, was now dead. Thomas was now made joint custodian with the Duke of Gloucester of the captive king, and, on the death of Gloucester, sole custodian. He was appointed Governor of the Tower of London, to which that king was then committed, and it is probable that when the king was removed to Pontefract Castle he was still in Earl Thomas's custody. With the mysterious end and disappearance of King Richard II we may or may not assume that Earl Thomas was not unacquainted; but it is certain, at any rate, that during his journey from Chester to London in the first place the captive king was subjected to harsh treatment.

Henry, Duke of Lancaster was crowned king on 13 October 1399, under the title of Henry IV. He created Earl Thomas Knight of the Bath, and summoned him to serve in his hereditary capacity of Chief Butler, an office which remains to this day the prerogative of the Earls of Arundel. Thomas was restored to all the honours and possessions of the Earldom of Arundel, and made it one of his first cares to build a sumptuous marble tomb in the church of the Augustinian Friars in Bread Street, where his father's remains had been interred.

Six years later he married Beatrix of Portugal, on 26 November 1405. The wedding took place in London in the presence of the king and queen, who were at the wedding feast. He took part in the king's wars against Owen Glendower in Wales, and supported Henry against the conspiracy of the Percys at his victorious Battle of Shrewsbury, and in his wars in France. When Henry V succeeded to the throne in 1413, Thomas was created Constable of Dover Castle, Warden of the Cinque Ports, and Lord High Treasurer of England. He joined the army

with which Henry V invaded France, and accompanied him
to Harfleur. Here he was taken ill with dysentry. He returned
to England and reached his castle at Arundel, where, his ill-
ness rapidly increasing, he shortly died, on the last day of
his thirty-fourth year, in the year 1415. He had no children
(Plan No. 1).

In the Lady Chapel is the tomb of John Fitzalan (6th Earl),
who died in 1421. A large table-tomb in Sussex marble, it is
raised on a step in the eastern part of the chapel. Earl John was
the second earl to be interred in the chapel. He was the cousin
of Earl Thomas above, and next in title, Thomas leaving no
direct heir. He was born in 1387, and died in 1421. He lies
buried with his wife Eleanor in front of the altar to Our Lady in
the Lady Chapel, his tomb of Purbeck marble still retaining one
brass ornament, representing the Fitzalan horse. It seems
probable that Earl John built or completed the Lady Chapel,
but no record has been preserved. (Plan No. 2.)

Intermural Tomb (Plan No. 3).—The remarkably fine tomb
of John, the 7th Earl (d. 1435) is in the wall, specially cut
away for its reception, between the choir and Lady Altar.
The slab rests on a double row of three open arches, with
one at the ends. On a lower slab in the enclosure thus formed
is the effigy of a shrouded emaciated corpse (cadaver),
representing the sculptor's interpretation of the post-mortal
state of the warrior whose living image is on the slab above.
The latter figure, like the rest of the tomb, in alabaster, is
represented in full plate armour with the Fitzalan horse
crouching at the feet. Note the plate armour of the Lancastrian type with a close-fitting tabard, showing arms of
Fitzalan quartering Maltravers, with short sleeves. The gorget
is of plate armour. The statue was originally painted, some
slight traces of which remain. This curious form of tomb
occurs in other places, notably in Winchester Cathedral
and Tewkesbury Abbey. The two figures were intended
to contrast man in the pride and pomp of his life and in
the decay and loathsomeness of death. At Tewkesbury Abbey
the cadaver is shown decaying, and being devoured by
lizards and snails. It has also been explained that the monuments were erected during the liftime of the person whom

they commemorated; the corpse being to remind him of his mortality; after burial this was removed, or placed below the actual effigy. Sometimes, however, the individual was buried elsewhere (as at Tewkesbury), or his executors did not complete the monument, the cadaver remaining in the place of honour.

The Earl John whom this tomb commemorates was the eldest son of the John Fitzalan buried in the Lady Chapel. He was born in 1408. He greatly distinguished himself in the French wars of the 15th century, and assisted in capturing Joan of Arc. While besieging the Castle of Gerberoi he was wounded by a cannon ball, one of his legs being shattered. He was taken prisoner and removed to Beauvais, where he died on 12 June 1435. He was buried in that city in the church of the Grey Friars, and the monument to his memory was put up by his wife· in this chapel. He, however, had willed his body to be buried here in this spot.

Some 400 years later, in 1855, a passage was noticed in the will of Fulke Eyton (a gentleman of a Shropshire family), who had been in the service of the Earls of Arundel. This will was dated 1451, and in its reference was made to a sum of money owing by the then Earl of Arundel for the deliverance out of the Frenchmen's hands, and for the carriage out of France of the bones of his brother, Lord John, which were to be buried in Arundel chapel, 'after his intent', when the debt was paid.

In November 1857 Canon Tierney obtained permission to search underneath the monument, which up to then had been looked upon as being only a cenotaph. There he found a skeleton with the bones of one leg missing. This was presumed to be the skeleton of Earl John, it being considered probable that the leg, which is known to have been badly damaged by a culverin, had been amputated in an attempt to save life, and that the body had been translated to Arundel in due course in accordance with the testator's request.

There is no record of the burial or tomb of Earl John's son, Earl Humphrey, who died a boy in 1438, aged nine years.

South Chantry.—Earl Humphrey was succeeded by his paternal uncle, Earl William (9th Earl), who died in 1488. (Plan No. 4.)

His tomb, and that of his wife, Joan, daughter of Richard Neville, and sister of the Earl of Warwick, the 'King-maker', is in the renowned south chantry, which by some is thought to be the finest medieval chantry-tomb in England. The details of the rich tracery, as also the buttressed pinnacles above the brattishing, will be easily discernible; likewise the ogee-canopied arches and twisted marble shafts. Of the whole composition there is a certain gracefulness which cannot be gainsaid, but to those whose tastes lead them to prefer bolder outlines and greater simplicity of design it has an appearance of gaudiness. Inside are the chapel and table-tomb, which supports a traceries-sided cist on which rest the effigies carved in Caen stone. The tomb itself is in blue-grey Purbeck marble.

The space under the canopy is partly filled by the tomb, which serves as a pedestal for the effigies of the earl and countess, and as an altar for the celebration of Mass for the dead. The unusual feature of the candle-prickets on this altar is noteworthy. At the feet of the earl is the Fitzalan horse, and at those of the countess, the gryphon, the emblem of the Montagues, Earls of Salisbury. The shape of the head-dress of the countess is rare in marble as it is on brass. It is noteworthy for its decoration and the manner in which the coronet is introduced into it. The rich robe under the surcoat was once painted and gilt. Round the neck is a necklace of roses and suns (the badges of Edward IV and the Yorkist emblem), joined by oak leaves (the cognizance of the Fitzalans).

Earl William founded an Arundel altar with an Arundel Mass at Magdalen College, Oxford. He was the patron of Caxton, who had his printing press in the Almonry in Westminster Abbey. He died in 1488, aged seventy.

North Chantry.—The tomb in the north chantry opposite is of Thomas, 10th earl (d. 1524), where also is buried William, his son (d. 1544), and is a curious medley of styles indicative of the retrograde movement in ecclesiastical art by which this period is characterised (Plan No. 5). Four crudely carved pillars support the uncouth canopy and pediment, on which are carved shields supported by horses and displaying the arms of the families of Fitzalan, Maltravers, Percy, and others. On the panelled back also the horse and oak-spray of Fitzalan are prominent. Part of the roof of the canopy was damaged by an enemy bomb which fell just outside the chapel in the 1939-45 war.

Earl Thomas succeeded Earl William in 1488. He married Margaret Woodville, sister of the Queen of Edward IV, and lived more at Downley Park, Singleton, rather than at Arundel; he died at Downley October 1524, appointing Robert Sherburn, Bishop of Chichester, his executor. He was succeeded by his son William, who also lived chiefly at Downley, where he died January 1544. He was buried in the same tomb as his father. A brass plate placed on the wall at the back of this monument by Lord Lumley in 1596 records the marriages of these two earls. (The 16th-century tombs in Purbeck marble at Singleton church are thought to have been intended for Earls Thomas and William, but lie empty.)

Henry (12th Earl), the only son of Earl William, above, was the last of the Fitzalans (Plan No. 6). He succeeded to the title on the death of his father in 1544. In favour with Henry VIII, persecuted during the reign of Edward VI, in power during the reign of Queen Mary, and for a time held in esteem by Elizabeth, he died at Arundel House in the Strand on 24 February 1580. He is buried at the south end of the high altar, at the foot of the mural tablet which records his name and doings. His only son, Henry, who had died 30 June 1556, aged 18 years, was buried in the church of St. Gudule at Brussels.

The master who surrendered the college was Alan Percy, a maternal uncle of Earl Henry, and son of Henry, Earl of Northumberland. The letters patent, dated 26 December 1544, provide one of the few instances in which noblemen procured grants of land bequeathed by their ancestors to monasteries, the patronage of which was hereditary in their families (Dugdale).

The Vaults.—The earls of the Howard line are buried in the north and south vaults, entered on the north and south side respectively of the tomb of John (7th Earl). In the south vault under the high altar, where the late 16th duke is buried, the remains of St. Philip Howard once reposed, who was arraigned on a charge of treason under Elizabeth in 1589, was wrongly condemned, and imprisoned in the Tower of London, where he died in 1595. His body was removed from the chapel of St. Peter at Vincula in the Tower to the Fitzalan Chapel in 1624 by his widow, Anne, Countess of Arundel, and in 1971, after his canonisation (1970) it was again removed to a new shrine in Arundel cathedral. (Plan No. 7.) There are four monuments to members of the Howard family, many of whom are buried there: the large black marble erection which disfigures the centre of the Lady Chapel, beneath which is interred Lord Henry Thomas Howard, brother of Duke Bernard Edward, who died in 1824 (Plan No. 8); those in the South Chantry to Henry Granville, 14th Duke of Norfolk, and Minna his wife, parents of the 15th Duke (Plan No. 9); and the recent monument to the 15th Duke of Norfolk, in the centre of the chapel (Plan No. 10). Henry Fitzalan Howard, 15th Duke of Norfolk, was born in 1847, and succeeded to the title in 1860, when barely 13 years old. This Duke is largely responsible for the chapel as it is now seen. Bernard, 16th Duke, his son, succeeded in 1917, and his memorial plaque is on the north wall (Plan No. 11).

On the floor at the head of the monument to Thomas, Earl of Arundel, and Beatrix, his wife, is a slab of Sussex marble containing the brass to Thomas Salmon, a squire, who was usher to the chamber of Henry V, and his wife, Agnes, who was a Portuguese lady, and chief waiting-woman to the Countess Beatrix. Originally there was a figure of the husband under a canopy, but it and part of the inscription have disappeared. That of the wife and the other half of the inscription remain; she wears the Lancastrian Collar of SS, and has a heart-shaped head-dress; two lap-dogs are shown at her feet. The inscription originally was as follows: 'Hic jacet Thomas Salmon, Armiger, nup'vusher comé Dñi Henrici quinti, nup' regis Angliae, et Agnes vxor ejus, alias dict' D'Olyver nup' de Portugalia principal' nup' mulier illustris' D'ne Beatricis Comitesse Arundel et Surr; quiquidem Thomas obijt XXIII die mens' maii, Anno Dñi Millimo CCCCXXX; et p'd'ta Agnes obijt Penultimo die Mensis maii, Anno Dñi Millimo CCCCXVIII; quor animab' p'pietur Deus. Amen'. (Plan No. 12.)

South of the brass to Thomas Salmon and his wife is that to John Threele (who died 1465) and his wife, Jane Barttelot (died 1469). He was marshal of the household to William, Earl of Arundel; he is shown in armour, and wears the Yorkist collar of suns and roses (the only example in brass in Sussex). The figure of the wife has disappeared; she was handmaid to two Countesses of Arundel, Beatrix and Joan. (Plan No. 13.)

Canon Tierney, whom this brass commemorates, was private chaplain to the Duke of Norfolk and parish priest from 1825 to 1862. He was one of the most distinguished English ecclesiastics of his time. His diligence in research and his literary work earned for him a Fellowship of the Royal Society and a Fellowship of the Society of Antiquaries. He was made one of the first canons of the chapter of the newly-restored Catholic diocese of Southwark under Dr. Grant. (Plan No. 14.)

Also in the Lady Chapel is a brass (three-quarter length) to Robert Warde, who died in 1474. Inscription: 'Hic jacet Dominus Robertus Warde, qui obijt I I I° die Ap'lis Anno D'ni Millesimo CCCCLXXIIII cuj' aīe p'picietur Deus. Amen'. (Plan No. 15.)

In the Lady Chapel is a brass to John Baker, a fellow of the College (died 1455); it shows him vested for Mass—that is, alb, amice, stole, maniple, and chasuble. His initials appear on the orphrey of the chasuble. On a label issuing from his mouth is the prayer 'Miserere mei Deus'. The inscription is missing. It read: 'Hic jacet Dn'us Johès Baker nup' socius hujus collegii qui obijt XV die Martii Ao Dni MCCCCLV, cujus, aie p'picietur Deus. Amen.' (Plan No. 16.)

In the Lady Chapel is a brass to a priest, Esperaunce Blondel, rector of Sutton (about 1450). Inscription: 'His jacet D'nus Esperaunce Blondel q'ndā rector eccl'ie de Sutton: cuj'aie p'picietur De'. Amen'. (Plan No. 17.)

This brass commemorates William Whyte, second master of the college, who died in 1419; he wears an almuce over his cassock and surplice. The inscription, which has been removed, originally read: 'Hic jacet corpus humatum D'ni Will'i Whyte s' c'di Magr'i Huj' Coll. qui obijt XX die mensis Feb. A.D. MCCCCXIX . . . ac multa bona contulit huic collegio, cujus anime propitietur Dues. Amen'. (Plan No. 18.)

This half-length brass is of Adam Ertham, first master of the college, who died before 1383. He is shown in a choir

cope (cappa nigra) as for the sarum use. The inscription
which has been removed once reads: 'D'nus Adm̄ Ertham
p'm'estre d'cest college gist ycy: dieux de s'alme eyt m'cy.
Amen'. (Plan No. 19.)

The Roofs.—Reference has already been made to the main
roof and stalls. In form the roof is low-pitched and vaulted. The
bosses are mainly original, consisting of the usual designs—
angels, patriarchs, prophets and the like, and also lions' heads
and the Fitzalan horse and oak-spray. The old oak can be
distinguished by the traces of gilding which it bears and its
somewhat greyish tone. In the Lady Chapel the roof is flat
panelled oak and modern; but the corbel to the arches and
roof are noteworthy and interesting. In this chapel the stalls
are almost completely original (*c.* 1400). In the main chapel
they are mainly restorations—though very skilful and exact
restorations. Old has here been blended with new in a wonderful
manner, showing to full advantage the high relief delicately
carved, the almost pure Decorated tracery patterns, the
grotesques and misericords.

The East Window.[3]—The remarkably beautiful stained glass
window was installed by the 15th duke in 1891 and represents
the duke assisting, with his young son the Earl of Arundel,
at the Requiem Mass of his first wife, Duchess Flora (née
Hastings); this is the sacrifice of propitiation for the souls
in Purgatory (represented below) through the merits of Christ
crucified (represented above), where are also figures of the
Blessed. In the central part are those ancestors conspicuous
for their good works and sanctity.

Although this window was not installed until 1891 it represents to some degree the window that existed up until the 17th
century. In the British Museum (MS. No. 1076 of the Harleian
Collection) is a document drawn up by John Withie of the
College of Arms in 1634 depicting the original window as it
existed then. John Withie was simply carrying out a routine
examination as part of the Heralds' visitation of Sussex[4]—this
meant recording coats of arms of claimants and on church
monuments. Six of the seven lights were nearly perfect when
John Withie called, and contained seven earls of Arundel and
six countesses—whom the members of the college were wont

to pray for in their daily prayers. Each earl bears his arms on his surcoat starting with Richard, third earl, and father of the founder and his second wife, Eleanor Plantagenet; Richard, fourth earl, the founder and Elizabeth de Bohun, his second wife; Thomas, fifth earl, and his wife Princess Beatrix of Portugal (glass broken); John, sixth earl, and Eleanor Berkeley, his wife; John, seventh earl, and Maud Lovel his wife; and William, ninth earl (the eighth earl died in infancy) and Lady Joan Nevill, his wife; and Thomas, tenth earl, and Margaret Widvile, his wife. Beside these portraits the window contained shields of arms depicting Richard, Earl of Cambridge; Henry, Duke of Lancaster; the arms of England; Pedro III, King of Castile, married to Constance, daughter of Edward III; and Thomas of Woodstock, Duke of Gloucester. Beside these shields were the arms of Aragon, Portugal, the earls and their wives and various Archbishops of Canterbury, including Thomas Bourchier, John Merton, and William Warham. An original piece of the window depicting Thomas Bouchier is all that survives of this original window, and is in the Duke of Norfolk's possession.

Those Buried in the Fitzalan Chapel
(as recorded in the Arundel Cathedral Bead Roll[5])

1382.—Ertham, Sir Adam.
1415.—Fitzalan, Earl Thomas. (13 October.)
1418.—Salmon, Agnes.
1419.—White, Dom. William. (20 February.)
1421.—Fitzalan, Earl John I.
1430.—Salmon, Thomas.
1435.—Fitzalan, Earl John II. (12 June.)
1439.—Fitzalan, Beatrice (wife of Earl Thomas). (23 October.)
1446.—Threel, John.
1456.—Baker, Dom John (Rev.).
1474.—Warde, Dom Robert (Rev.).
1488.—Fitzalan, Earl William.
        Fitzalan, Joan.
        Blondel, Dom Esperaunce (Rev.). (No date to be found.)
1511.—Mundy, Dom John (Rev.).
1524.—Fitzalan, Earl Thomas. (October.)

1580.—**Fitzalan**, Earl Henry. (Last of the Fitzalans persecuted during the reign of Edward VI.) (24 February.)
1595.— **Howard**, Philip (Saint). (Interred in the Tower) (Since transferred to Cathedral Shrine on 10 March 1971.) (19 October.)
1624.—**Howard**, Philip (Saint) (translation of relics to Fitzalan Chapel)
1630.—**Anne**—Countess of Arundel. (Wife of St. Philip.) (Vault under Lady Chapel.) (19 April.)
1860.—**Norfolk**, Henry Charles Granville. (Duke of Norfolk.) (25 November.)
1862.—**Tierney**, V. Rev. Canon Mark Aloysius. (19 February.)
      Hope Scott, Catherine Mary. (6 June.)
1868.—**Hope**, Philip James. (9 April.)
1877.—**Maxwell**, three infants: Faith, Hope and Charity. (Spring.)

From the Fitzalan Chapel Register[6]

1886.—The Most Noble Augusta Mary Minna Catherine. (Duchess Dowager of Norfolk.) (31 March.)
1887.—The Most Noble Flora Paulyna Hetty Barbara. (Duchess of Norfolk. (19 April.)
      Bickerton, Richard, Pernell. (Viscount Lyons.) (10 December.)
1889.—**Stewart**. (Infant daughter of Dr. and Lady Philippa Stewart.) (28 December.)
1892.—The Most Eminent and Most Reverend Edward Cardinal Howard, Bishop of Frascati. (27 September.)
1899.—**Fitzalan Howard**, The Lady Margaret. (17 November.)
1902.—**Fitzalan Howard**, Philip Joseph Mar. (Earl of Arundel.) (14 July.)
1917.—**Fitzalan Howard**, The Most Noble Henry. (15th Duke of Norfolk, E.M., K.G. (15 February.)
1925.—**Fitzalan Howard**, The Lady Mary Adeliza. (28 February.)
1975.—**Fitzalan Howard**, The Most Noble Bernard Marmaduke. (16th Duke of Norfolk, E.M., K.G., G.C.V.O.) (6 February.)

Saint Edmund, King and Martyr[7]

On this 10th day of March 1971, the box containing the reputed relics of Saint Edmund, King and Martyr, was taken from the Reliquary in the private Chapel of Arundel Castle, and placed in a new Casket of Oak, the former container being in a decayed and very fragile condition.

The remains were then taken to the Fitzalan Chapel and placed in the Vault near the High Altar of the former Collegiate Church of the Holy Trinity.

The removal took place on the instructions and authority of The Most Noble Bernard Marmaduke, 16th Duke of Norfolk, by the Very Reverend Canon Christopher Aston, Administrator of the Cathedral Church at Arundel, assisted by Mr. Lawson Paul (Architect), Mr. Francis Steer (Archivist), and Mr. T. A. Healey.

T. A. Healey
Asst. Agent to the Duke of Norfolk

Saint Philip Howard[8]

Born 28th June 1557   Died in Tower of London 19th October 1595

The Relics were translated from the Vault near the High Altar of the Collegiate Church of the Holy Trinity at Arundel to a newly constructed SHRINE in the CATHEDRAL CHURCH OF ARUNDEL on the 10th day of March 1971.

T. A. Healey
Asst. Agent to the Duke of Norfolk

Noates taken in Arundell Church in the tyme of
the Visitacon of Sussex · 1634 · It me
Jo: Withie

The portratures of divers of the Earles of
Arundell sett up in the Glasse window in the
High Chancell & their Countisses, for
whom the religiues in the   adioyning
did remember in their dayly Devotions as
their foundors.

Page 68. A section of John Withie's sketch of the East window of the Fitzalan Chapel in 1634, before its final destruction. The founding Earl is depicted on the left of the second row.

Page 69. The restored window commemorating Flora, Duchess of Norfolk, wife of the 15th Duke (who restored the Fitzalan Chapel) based on the original designs sketched by John Withie. The founding Earl is shown at the base of the second light from the left.

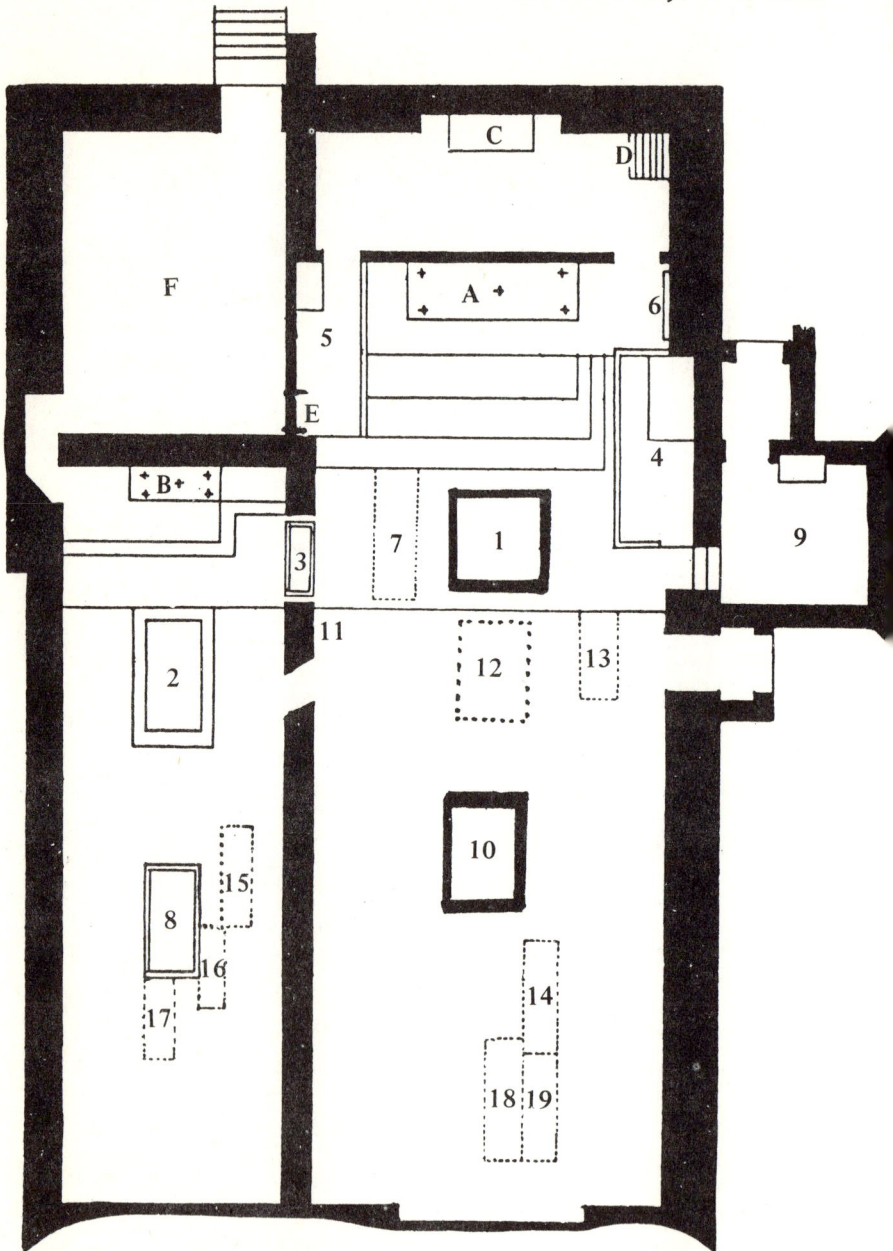

THE FITZALAN CHAPEL: KEY PLAN

A   Original high altar   E   Entrance to Sacristy
B   Original Lady altar   now stopped up
C   Master's private altar   F   Sacristy
D   Night stairs to Master's Lodging

Chapter XII

Epilogue

THE DIVISION OF PARISH CHURCH AND COLLEGE CHAPEL

THE OLD PARISH CHURCH of Arundel is probably the only church building in the country to encompass two distinct places of worship with two dedications and each served by two different denominations. This situation has existed since 1544 when Henry VIII conveyed the chancel of the church, with all its possessions, to Henry, 12th Earl of Arundel. Earl Henry desired to retain the chancel, known as the Fitzalan Chapel, because apart from being his family's mortuary chapel it was the private chapel of the college of the Holy Trinity, which upon its dissolution he acquired from the king for the promised sum of 1,000 marks.

Thus from the end of the 14th century two distinct places of worship existed within the compass of the parish church, the high altar serving the College of Secular Canons within the Fitzalan Chapel, and the altar of St. Nicholas serving the parishioners (situated in the south transept), the division indicated by the 14th-century wrought-iron grille. So distinct were these two situations that documentary evidence records the chapel of St. Nicholas being called 'the Parish Chancel', although architecturally it formed the south transept. This, of course, did not prevent parishioners hearing Mass when said at the high altar, the fine pulpit being so constructed that a cleric could direct people's attention as to what was going on beyond the grille.

At the dissolution of the religious houses under Henry VIII, in the middle of the 16th century, the peaceful existence of this foundation and its separate congregations became drastically altered. Services were maintained in the church of St. Nicholas, but the Fitzalan Chapel, apart from the interment of members of the Fitzalan family, fell into disuse. Thus, despite neglect, the purpose of the chapel as the tomb-house of the Earls of Arundel and their heirs, the Dukes of Norfolk continued, as the registers testify. In 1643 even the worship in St. Nicholas's was disrupted when the parliamentary troops marched into the town and used the church as a barracks, the Fitzalan Chapel fared no better in being used as a stable for their horses. The stained glass was smashed throughout, and many statues and frescos suffered irreparable damage.

Subsequent to this period, for 150 years the Fitzalan Chapel remained in a ruined state. The existing damage was extended when in 1782 the roof was allowed to be dismantled and fall on the tombs below, a slate roof being erected in its stead. Between 1837 and 1844 the 12th and 13th Dukes of Norfolk made a concerted effort at restoring the Fitzalan Chapel, and in 1874 St. Nicholas church was restored as well.

The division of church and chapel became a subject of public interest when in March 1879 the Anglican vicar brought a lawsuit against the 15th Duke of Norfolk, claiming the Fitzalan Chapel as the chancel of St. Nicholas church. The duke, a Roman Catholic, won the case, and having built a brick wall on the Fitzalan Chapel side of the iron grille, established the right thus to maintain the privacy of his own private chapel. The duke offered to have the vicar's side of the wall faced with plaster, but the vicar refused. This state of affairs remained until the 1950s when the section of the wall above the level of the rood beam was removed and replaced with glass. In March 1969 Bernard, the 16th Duke of Norfolk, desiring to have a view of the Fitzalan Chapel from the nave of St. Nicholas's, in the interests of Christian unity, gave permission to have the remaining section of wall demolished. The view remained partially obstructed, however, by the beautiful altar and reredos erected across the intervening space by Sir Gilbert Scott in 1872. Duke Bernard had obviously no wish to interfere with this arrangement, but in 1975 he died and the Anglican congregation elected to adopt a sanctuary scheme, with a clearer view of the chapel, in his memory. The Fitzalan Chapel to date is used regularly about five or six times a year, and is likely in the future to be in daily use, subsequent to the establishment of almshouses in the old college buildings to be maintained by the Sovereign Military and Hospitaller Order of St. John, of Jerusalem, Rhodes and Malta.

Lord Chief Justice Coleridge in the course of his judgment in the case of 1879 said that he hoped 'some solution might be arrived at which, while preserving for the Duke of Norfolk all the rights in this building (Fitzalan Chapel) which he would care to preserve, might obtain for the parish all such use of it as would be of any benefit to them'. This has to some extent been fulfilled since the commencement of regular public Mass for the parish in the chapel from 1 April 1886 (on the day of the burial of Minna, Duchess of Norfolk, wife of the 14th duke) to the present day, and the recent (25 January 1977) combined ecumenical service, in which the wrought iron grille proved to be no obstacle to Christian unity. Indeed, the 24 May 1980 commemorated the sixth centenary of the foundation of church, college and chapel, or more appropriately the feast of Corpus Christi which in 1980 fell on 5 June, and was fittingly celebrated by the Knights of Malta with the Catholic and Anglican parishioners of Arundel in the traditional solemn procession of the Blessed Sacrament through the town. It was on that day that the Knights as the new tenants of the priory decided on Corpus Christi (18 June) 1981 for the official opening of the priory as an almshouse of the Order.

Number I: Précis

LICENCE FOR THE FOUNDATION OF ARUNDEL COLLEGE

N.B. Count in this document should more correctly be translated as 'Earl'.

1 April Westminster: m.12. 1380

Licence for 40 l. paid to the King for his kinsman, Richard, Earl of Arundel and Surrey, in fulfilment of the purpose of his father, Richard, the late earl, to annul the Priory of Arundel, subject to the alien abbey of Seez in France, and found a chantry or college in the parish church of St. Nicholas, Arundel, without the castle, on condition that the master and chaplains thereof pay to the King 20 marks yearly during the war with France.

The Collegiate Church of Arundel in the County of Sussex: The King's licence for its foundation and gift. (Patent Rolls, 3 Richard, part 3, membrane 12.)

The King to all those etc. greetings:

One of our faithful kinsmen, Richard, Count (Earl) of Arundel and Surrey, one of the executors of the will of his father, the late Count of Arundel and Surrey, has petitioned us as to the following matter: as his father had said during his life-time and most happily recorded in his final testament, he proposed to establish a foundation in perpetuity of a chantry of six chaplains to serve God there below his castle of Arundel. To this end no change will be made in this provision, unless by adding improvement to bring about more effectively and perseveringly its fulfilment, given the way of the mortal world, by the will of God, entry into these rights will take place. And the present Count, saying, concerning the implementation of his co-executorship of the aforesaid will, considering the aforesaid chantry, if it were to be found below the said castle it would not endure in perpetuity by reason of the likelihood of certain conditions, and heartily desirous of holding to the aforesaid intention of his father and the increase in devotion which ought to be brought about, [that he] intended to be found and establish the said chantry or college in the parish church of St. Nicholas Arundel without the said castle. [The said church] is now a priory of the monks of the order of St. Benedict, subject in perpetuity to the alien priory of Seez in France, and from which priory 20 marks yearly are due to us by

74

occasion of the state of war between us and those of France. Nonetheless, in fulfilment of the aforesaid will of the late Count, his father, the [present count] begged licence of us, and the will and consent of all others concerned in this intervention. We wish to make known our royal licence concerning this purpose. The advowson of the said priory, which by the death of our dearest lord and father, Edward, late Prince of Wales, [that advowson] amongst other of his possessions was left to him and to his heirs as it might be said, and according to his bequest falls to us by the law of inheritance. Considering that the said priory was founded and ordained by the ancestors of the said count, and in which priory were one prior and a few monks, [sometimes three, sometimes four or more] the said priory would be preserved, and thus according to the original foundation of the same priory, no more than a total number of five monks would be maintained. And that all others, with the consent of the said prior, would therefore be withdrawn, so that the priory itself would not become desolate and enter into decline, and that divine service would not cease. As the aforesaid present Count gives and concedes, as much in the interest of his own proposal for the future as for the will of his said father, according to his intention, having and holding for himself and his heirs, the advowson of the same church, a tax of twenty-one marks and a valor of twenty pounds per annum, to us and to our heirs, within our kingdom of England, by the award of the present Count or his heirs, granted and assigned in perpetuity.

And also concerning the expression of our grace, conceding and giving licence to the prior and to the religious house of the aforesaid priory, together with all its manors, lands, tenements and other temporal possessions, as well as whatsoever pertains to the said priory with its appurtenances, not least being the advowson of the said church of St. Nicholas Arundel, to the rectory of which, as a habitation, and where the now aforesaid priory will be situated, according to the original intention of the foundation, the prior and religious house of the said priory will be moved. And the advowsons of the churches of Yabetone, Rustystone, Billyngeshurst, Kerredeford, Cockyng and the church of Hamptone, and as well a tenth coming from certain lands and tenements in Prestone, Gorynge, Hertynge, Bourne and Storghton; which said churches and tenths the same prior and religious house at present hold for their own use as has been stated, and the advowsons of the vicar of Kerredeford will be given and conceded to the aforesaid present Count, to have and to hold for himself and his heirs, from us and our heirs and other chief lords of that fief (in respect thereof) will be given and conceded in perpetuity. And the same present Count, when he has received from the aforesaid prior and religious house the said manors etc. for himself and his heirs, they may be transmitted as holdings and possessions in perpetuity, and removed from the authority and will of the aforesaid abbot of Seez and of the religious house of the same place, and with the consent of all others having suit in that matter, with that of the aforesaid prior and monks, so that the same priory, being annulled, it will be possible to found and establish in the place where the said priory now is, a chantry or college, and following the proposal of the aforesaid late Count, six secular priests; and increasing them with seven other secular priests to the number of thirteen, of whom one shall take precedence over the others and who will be called the Master.

And in this fashion, the said present Count wishes to impose the name of the chantry or college. In the aforesaid church of St. Nicholas Arundel, the priests will celebrate divine service, for the welfare of our estate and that of the said present Count, while we live, and for our souls when we depart from this light, and for the soul of the said present Count, and for the souls of our ancestors and of those of our heirs and for those of the late Count and of the present Count, and according to the original purpose of the foundation of the said priory, Mass will be celebrated daily, according to and following the limitations, dispositions, orders and statutes made by the present Count in this matter in perpetuity. And that the present Count himself, as well as the said manors, lands, tenements and whatsoever temporal possessions, the aforesaid advowsons of the churches, tenths and revenues of the said vicarage will be within his power to give and to assign to the aforesaid Master and chaplains, once having founded and established the said chantry or college, the said Master and chaplains and their successors as Master and chaplains, having and holding the said chantry or college from the aforesaid present Count and from his heirs freely and in perpetuity as a frankalmoign.

We direct with forethought that the performance of such pious works and meritorious acts be carried out according to the pious proposal of the late Count and the commendable intention of the aforesaid present Count, whom we wish to support effectively; to this end, the same Count will pay to us the sum of forty pounds. Wishing graciously that the aforesaid payment be yearly, we give and bestow upon the aforesaid present Count the advowson of the aforesaid priory, to have and to hold for himself and for his heirs, of us and of our heirs through tenure, which in respect thereof ought to be customary and in perpetuity. We further give and bestow upon the same Count as mentioned from us and from our heirs, the aforesaid advowsons of the churches with their valors and taxes.

And we further graciously concede and give licence from us and from our heirs, as much as is within our power [to do so] to the said prior and religious house that same manor of Yabetone, with appurtenances and one house-site [tenant] 100 acres of land, 6 acres of meadowland, 12 acres of woodland and 15 shillings rent with appurtenances in Arundel; 60 acres of land with appurtenances called Roseresland in Billyngshurst; 16 shillings rent with appurtenances in Cokynge; 40 pounds and 10 shillings rent with appurtenances in Rogate; 40 shillings rent with appurtenances in Chichester; as well as 20 shillings annual rent or 20 shillings annual pension levied on the cathedral church of Chichester through the churches of Sengletone and Eastdene. And as well the advowsons of the

said church of St. Nicholas Arundel, and the advowsons of the said
churches of Yabetone, Rustitone, Billyngeshurst, Kerredeford, Cockyng
and the church of Hampton, and the tenths from the said vicarages.
Together with the tenths of the churches, the manors, house-site, land,
meadow- and wood-land, and the rent or pensions with appurtenances
and the advowsons forming an integral part of the aforesaid priory, and
whatsoever might be said to belong to the same priory and may be
granted, bestowed and alienated to the present Count, to have and to hold
etc. and to that same present Count belongs the same manors, house-site,
land, meadow- and wood-land and rent or pensions together with all
appurtenances and advowsons and whatsoever belongs to the aforesaid
priory, which may be called temporal goods, which he wishes to acquire
from the aforesaid prior and religious house to receive and to hold for
himself and his heirs according to the aforesaid form in perpetuity, and
that the same Count, having therein full and peaceful seisin, and the
aforesaid prior and monks, through the disappropriation of the aforesaid
priory and with the authority and consent of all those concerned, and
having dispensed with troublesome matters, and that the present priory
might be annulled, and [refounded] established as promised in the
aforesaid place where the present priory stands as a perpetual chantry or
college of thirteen secular priests, one of whom is to take precedence over
the others and is to be called the Master. And the same present Count is
thus licensed to select the name of the chantry or college: and to provide
for the rule of the aforesaid Master and priests, who will be there with
the foundation, that as aforesaid, divine service will be held in the aforesaid church of St. Nicholas for our welfare and that of the present Count,
while we live, and for our soul when we depart from this light, and for
the soul of the aforesaid late Count and for the souls of our ancestors and
for those of our heirs, and those of the late Count and of the present
Count, and according to the purpose of the original foundation of the
aforesaid priory, they will celebrate Mass according to and within the
limitations, provisions, ordinances and statutes made by the present Count
in this matter in perpetuity.

And that the same aforesaid present Count, to whom the manors,
house-site, land, meadow- and wood-land and rent or pension with appurtenances and the aforesaid advowsons and whatsoever other temporal
possessions now belong to the aforesaid priory and acquiring, receiving
and obtaining [these possessions] to have and to hold for himself and
his heirs, may give and bestow upon the aforesaid Master and chaplains
of the aforesaid chantry or college to have and to hold of themselves,
the present Count and of his heirs, freely and in perpetuity as a frankalmoign, and that divine service be performed according to the aforesaid
terms. And that the same Master and chaplains, as well as the same
manors, house-site, land, meadow- and wood-land, and rent or pensions
with appurtenances and the advowsons, and all the aforesaid temporal
possessions [they] will have and receive according to the aforesaid
agreement above written, and in so much as the aforesaid churches of

St. Nicholas Arundel and the churches of Yabetone, Rustytone, Billinges-
hurst and Kerredeford and the aforesaid church of Hampton and all the
parts thereof, as well spiritual as otherwise and whatsoever now belongs
to the aforesaid priory he will take unto himself and will thus be able
to appropriate and to hold for his own use and that of his aforesaid heirs
and successors, so that the aforesaid divine service may be celebrated in
perpetuity from thenceforward in full and entire appropriation, just as the
aforesaid prior and religious house now hold the churches, tenths, and
spiritual rights and fully retain other of the aforesaid temporal possessions.
We wish that the aforesaid Master and chaplains and their successors
preaching in the aforesaid church of St. Nicholas Arundel where the
said priory now stands, will inhabit the present house as their abode in
perpetuity. And that the aforesaid abbot and religious house of Sees
will be removed from the aforesaid donations, concessions, alienations and
assignations of the aforesaid prior and monks without compensation or
restitution. Further the annulment of the aforesaid priory is to be
approved, ratified, confirmed or accepted, and all the aforesaid manors,
house-site, fields, woodland and rents or pensions with appurtenances
and advowsons, churches and tithes as above indicated which now belong
to the said priory, are conceded to the Master and chaplains, and their
right and claim totally confirmed, and whatsoever rights the aforesaid
abbot and religious house of Sees has or will have therein will thenceforth
be bestowed on him [the present Count] and upon his successors, and
will be given and released to the aforesaid Master and chaplains and their
aforesaid successors, and they may make their home in quiet and
perpetuity in whatsoever manner and fashion may be suitable or
indicated. And that therefore, the aforesaid Master and chaplains and
their aforesaid successors will be secure in perpetuity concerning all
and singular of the abovesaid manors, house-site, land, meadow- and
wood-land and rent or pensions with appurtenances and the aforesaid
advowsons and tenths which now belong to the said priory without
interference or disturbance from the aforesaid abbot and religious house
or their successors. And the aforesaid abbot and religious house and their
successors will be excluded by penalty in perpetuity from tenure which
we bestow similarly by special licence and by statute of the land in
mortmain which cannot be changed etc. or impeded etc. In whom etc.

The King at Westminster, the first day of April

Number II: Licence from the King to expand the same College
(Patent Rolls 5 Richard II, p. 1 membrane 3.)

The King to all those etc. greetings:

Know that when our very dear lord and uncle Edward, Late King of
England now dead, conceded by his letters patent and gave licence from
him and from his heirs, as much as lay within his powers, to Richard, then
Count of Arundel, for the same Count to give and to concede to certain

chaplains and clerics, for the foundation of the then former chapel below his castle of Arundel an annual rent of 107 marks collected from his manors of Angmeryng, Wepham, and Warnecamp in the county of Sussex, the same chaplains and clerics to have and to hold for themselves and their successors, and which the same late Count or his heirs would give to the aforesaid chaplains and clerics, lands, tenements, and rents to the value of the said 107 marks yearly, having and holding for themselves and their heirs in perpetuity, according to the full force of the letters patent of our uncle. And afterwards, through our letters patent, we conceded by our special favour and gave licence from us and from our heirs within the scope of our powers, to our dear and faithful kinsman, Richard, his son, now Count of Arundel; further, the said rent he may give and concede to the aforesaid chaplains and clerics a yearly rent of 24 and 15 marks collected from his manors of Pipering, Southstoke, Tortyngtone, and Up-Merdon in the said county, having and holding for themselves and their heirs in aid of their welfare, which the same present Count, his heirs or executors will give to the same chaplains and clerics, lands and tenements to the value of the said 24 and 15 marks yearly as stated fully in our same letters patent. And now the same present Count as stated, with our licence founded in the said place a chantry or college of one Master and 12 chaplains within the parish church of Arundel. We, to the supplication of the same present Count, concede and give licence from us and our heirs, within the scope of our power, to the same present Count, that the same said annual rent of 107 marks with the aforesaid 24 and 15 marks yearly as abovesaid, he may give and assign to the same Master and chaplains of the same college; to have and collect yearly; *viz*: the said 107 marks of the aforesaid manors of Angmeryng, Wepham and Warnecamp, and the said 24 and 15 marks from the aforesaid manors off Piperyng, Southstoke, Cortyngtone, and Up-Merdone to the same Master and chaplains of the said college and to their successors and that the said present Count and his heirs or successors will give and assign to the same Master and chaplains of the said college, lands, tenements, rents and advowsons to the value of the aforesaid rent, having and holding for themselves and their successors in perpetuity, according to the abovesaid form; So that for ever after, the said lands, tenements, rents and advowsons or parcels thereof, will be given and assigned to the same Master and chaplains of the aforesaid college as aforesaid. That then in so much as the same lands, tenements, rents and advowsons amount to 107 marks yearly and 24 and 15 marks yearly as abovesaid. And the same Master and chaplains of the aforesaid college will be able to receive and to hold from the aforesaid present Count the same said yearly rent etc, having and collecting yearly in the aforesaid manner, by the said Master and chaplains of the said college and their successors, which the same present Count, his heirs or executors will give and assign to the aforesaid Master and chaplains of the aforesaid college, lands, tenements, rents and advowsons to the value aforesaid, having and holding for themselves and their successors, in perpetuity, according to the aforesaid form as aforesaid.

We thus give special immediate licence to be held in mortmain by the statutes of the land, and not to be changed or obstructed.

The King, Westminster, 7 day of December

Cal. Patent Rolls, 1377-81, p. 494, pat. 3. Richard ii pt. iij m 12.
(Printed in Dugdale's *Monasticon Anglicanum* vj., p. 1377.)

APPENDIX II

THE COLLEGIATE INVENTORY OF 1517

The inventory is dated 1 October 1517 and begins with a list of books.

Twelve misals or mass-books are recorded, four of which had musical settings, one of them being described as a 'New Massebooke . . . the gift of Sir William Wight late Maister . . .' (he died in 1421). Another of the new mass-books was presented by Sir Adam Smith, sub-master, for use in the shrine chapel of 'our Lady over the Gate'. (The old town gate which spans the original London road, but was incorporated into the castle grounds by the 15th duke.) Another mass-book was presented by Sir Thomas Dene to the fraternity of St. Christopher and given to the college for safe keeping. (The high altar of the parish church was dedicated to St. Christopher. This altar was in the south transept or at the head of the south aisle as the college chapel occupied the site of the chancel and the fraternity was a sort of altar society.)

There are also recorded a 'gospeller' and a 'pisteler', books containing the Gospel and epistle readings. Four lectionaries or 'legends', as they were called, come next. These were readings for the office of matins, and included passages of Scripture, lists of the saints and the writings of the fathers. Two portoses are included—which were probably breviaries (books for the personal use of the clergy containing matins, the night office, and the day hours). Three more breviaries are included with a collection of seven antiphoners and two ledgers. (The antiphoners contained the antiphons, initatories, hymns, collects and psalms, with their respective musical settings—excluding the office of matins. The ledgers were large office books for exclusive use in choir, *cf.* the Carthusian tradition to this day.) One of the antiphoners was given by Beatrice, Countess of Arundel, and three breviaries (or portoses) are described at the time of the inventory as being one in the possession of the vicar and one at the Earl of Arundel's hunting lodge of Downley in Singleton, and the third being the gift of Sir John Colmorde, former master of the college. The list of books also includes three manuals, three martyrologies, one collectar, a psalter, ten grails and two ordinals (collectars contained the collects, grails or graduals the musical setting of the Mass and ordinals were the instructions on the divine office, two of these were a gift from William White, master). Fourteen processionals were also included containing music and rubrics for processions, two of these were at Downley. Sundry other books are mentioned, including a Bible used for reading in the refectory.

Among other objects are listed a heart of silver gilt and seven tabernacles. These latter were reliquaries, one containing a relic of the true cross, one a bone of St. Lawrence, and one the relics of St. Etheldreda. Mention is also made of a relic of the table from the Last Supper.

There are also listed objects described as 'tablets'. These were probably paxbredes which served for the kiss of peace—a representation of our Lord's passion being kissed by celebrant and congregation in turn. Three of these contained relics, one of a thorn from the crown of our Lord, and two of the Blessed Virgin Mary.

Six crucifixes are recorded, one containing another relic of a thorn. Among the statues are included the Holy Trinity with a bone of St. Stephen hanging from it, St. John of Beverly likewise with a bone of the Saint, St. Peter and St. Paul, and an angel bearing numerous relics.

Next are listed the chalices, eight in all with patens, one being given by Joan, Countess of Arundel, the mother of Earl William. Two were for St. Christopher's altar in the parish church. Two paxbredes are mentioned by name, including a great 'owche' packed with stones—this must refer to a brooch or morse used as a cope clasp. Five pairs of basins are recorded, one presented by Joan, Countess of Arundel, and one by William Rede, Bishop of Chichester. Candlesticks are listed in six pairs and one single 'round one', and two large round ones to stand before the altar.

Thirty-one rings for 'rydelles' are listed—these were to hang the dorsal curtains from the riddle posts around the altar. Cruets for water and wine and sacring bells follow with seven censers, an incense boat, three holy water buckets with sprinklers, two silver scallop shells for mixing salt into holy water, and three crowns of silver and gilt, two for the statue of our Lady in 'Mary-gate' and one for a statue of our Lord.

An altar slab is mentioned and two cloths for the high altar and a frontal of gold. Two albs, two amices, two 'fanons' (maniples), and a stole, together with two albs and two amices for crucifers. Also listed are two altar cloths (more likely an altar cover) of blue velvet with gold embroidered eagles, a lavabo towel, three albs, three amices, three maniples, two stoles, a chasuble, two tunicles and seven copes. Two dorsal curtains are mentioned with a cover of cloth of gold, a lavabo towel, a frontal, three albs, three amices, two stoles, a cope, a 'corporas' (corporal), and a 'corporas case' (burse). Then two copes of cloth of gold, a cope of blue satin powdered with golden stars, two blue cloths of baudekin (a rich silk) embroidered with squirrels, birds and branches, a single chasuble, and a blue buckram altar cloth. Gifts of Thomas Salmon, Esquire, include a chasuble, stole, maniple, alb, amice and corporas case (burse), all apparently in blue damask with cloth of silver.

The list continues with a red altar cover embroidered with beasts, hawks' feet seizing the back of beasts, two palls, a frontal, a towel, three albs, three amices, three maniples ('favours'), two stoles, a chasuble, two tunicles, a burse and corporal, and three copes. Further to this is recorded an altar cover embroidered with gold lions, a frontal, towel, three albs, three amices, three maniples, two stoles, a chasuble, two tunicles, a cope, and two red curtains powdered with gold lions. Next comes a set of vestments of red velvet worked with a large lion of yellow velvet, including a chasuble, two tunicles, three albs, three amices, three maniples, two stoles and a cope. Then comes a set of red baudekin powdered with blue including altar cover, a frontal, towel, burse, three albs, three amices, three maniples, two stoles, and two copes. This is followed by a 'purple' set of vestments including chasuble, two dalmatics, three albs, three amices, three maniples, two stoles and a mantle (veil?), plus a frontal and two altar cloths. Then comes a red set of cloth of gold embroidered with crosses and three lions sharing one head! Three albs, three amices, three maniples, two stoles, a chasuble, two tunicles are included with yet another alb, amice, mantle (?), two copes, an altar cloth, a cloth of gold frontal and a towel. These were the vestments used for the celebration of the Holy Trinity, the college's dedication.

Following these comes a red altar cloth ('old red') with a frontal and towel, three albs, three amices, two stoles, two maniples, a chasuble, two tunicles and three copes. Then comes three copes of white damask for celebrant, deacon and sub-deacon.

The inventory then includes two red altar covers with a frontal of gold damask velvet. These were given to the college at the time of the burial of Beatrice, Countess of Arundel. These are followed by a set of vestments for high Mass (chasuble, dalmatic and tunicle) with 'whole apparel' (this could refer to aparelled albs and amices) plus a cope of the same. Two copes of red and black follow, with two of cloth of gold, one of plain red in rough velvet with blue 'orfrays' (orphries), then four copes of red silk for children (presumably for boy bishops). Then comes a green altar cover with frontal and towel which is said to be used for feasts of confessors (but yellow was more common for confessors in the English liturgical tradition). This is followed by copes and high Mass vestments of the same type together with altar cover, frontal, towel and another high Mass set with three copes all in green.

The next item is a 'sepulchre' which was probably a tabernacle for preserving the blessed sacrament, Easter Sepulchre (?) (the original type was a model of the church of the Holy Sepulchre in Jerusalem). This has its own 'canopy' or tabernacle veil. Another canopy ('seloure') was included with three pairs of curtains (dorsal), two altar cloths for a side altar, two cushions of white damask to support the Mass books (missals), a chasuble of white satin with a stole, maniple ('fanon') and 'apparel for alb', and an old transom.

Next occurs a white altar cover of gold stuff with two copes, and vestments and apparels for celebrant, deacon and sub-deacon (high Mass set), plus copes, all of the same white cloth of gold, including a cover and frontal for the high altar and another cover for the Lady altar, plus another five white copes, frontal and towel. Then comes another high Mass set in the same material with apparels and copes—the gift of Beatrice, Countess of Arundel.

The inventory then records a high Mass set, three copes and altar, altar cover and frontal, and besides another set of vestments and three more copes all in white. These were for feasts of our Lady and the Saturday commemoration. The list continues with three altar cloths, one with a red cross in the middle, a frontal, a towel, a chasuble, an alb, a maniple, two stoles, an amice (for Ember days), a cope of violet velvet worked with the arms of Mr. Dudley, a cope given by master John Doget, and a chasuble of blue with stole and maniple. (Edward Dudley was steward to the college during Doget's mastership.)

A further pair of altar cloths (covers) of blue and with rich orphries 'of nedill workes made by M. John Nele'. (John Neale was master before Doget.) A cope of red stuff with rich orphries likewise by the hand of master Neal is listed together with a gown of the Lady Maltravers (heaven knows how this came into the college's possession). Then are listed a chasuble of white damask, two burses, a coverlet given by John Warren ('alias Fy Hock', a former precentor), a burse (corporas case) of black velvet given by John Mundy, former sub-master, a plain black altar cover with a frontal and towel, plus three copes of the same and a high Mass set likewise, but somewhat decayed.

Then are listed a high Mass set of black velvet embroidered and apparelled. These were given by Beatrice, Countess of Arundel, complete with three albs of cloth of gold, and apparel, three stoles, three maniples, two amices, a girdle of silk, two cloths of gold baudekin, a cloth of baudekin with balls of gold, two cloths of bandekin with birds of gold, a cloth of gold baudekin with 'libardes' of gold with conics. Further to these are listed two cloths of bandekin with branches, with leaves of gold and green, a red cloth of baudekin with a water flower of gold with green leaves. A baudekin 'candell colome', two red cloths with gold beasts, a cloth of old russet velvet 3¼yds. in length and 2¼yds. in breadth. Next comes a sepulchre (tabernacle) in gold, a square yard of cloth of tissue with a frontal of the same An embroidered saddle-cloth is included, being of red velvet, which once belonged to Earl Thomas, since transformed into a chasuble. A square red canopy is listed as belonging to the sepulchre (tabernacle, ciborium, or pyx) as used for the feast of Corpus Christi. Eight pieces of tapestry are included for hanging in the choir, a chasuble, two tunicles of blue, two albs lacking apparels, a stole and a maniple. Then follows a set of white vestments for high Mass, a cloth of gold gown (given by Joan, Lady Maltravers) since made into a cope and chasuble. Also included is a gown of purple velvet presented by William, Earl of Arundel, son of Lady Maltravers, since made into a cope. Then comes a gown of black velvet presented by master John Neal, and four staffs with tips of silver for the use of the rectors.

The inventory concludes with a list of books in the college's possession. These works include *Pupilla Oculi*, a volume with the Acts of the Apostles with Apocolypse and the rule of the apostles. Other works include the four Gospels, a book on the Trinity, a book of sermons for all Marian feasts, two books of tracts and a description of the 'world'. Another work was devoted to the Acts of the Apostles and five volumes are described as 'Decretals'. The college library is also recorded as possessing a book on logic and one called *The constitutions of Otto and Ottobon*, a volume entitled *Vetus Pauperum*, a codex, and a *Nuguci* (possibly Hugocio's lexicon of grammatical derivations). Further books include *Sanctus Johannis Crisostimus* (St. John Crisostrom), and a book of Genesis and Exodus. Other works include *Parabole Salamonis*, a Bible, a Bible concordance, two psalters, the *Golden Legend* ('Legenda Aurea'). St. Thomas Aquinas on the articles of faith and the sacraments, and a book of sermons. Then comes *Manipulus Florum, Commune loquium Johannis Wellensis* and *Textus cum Elementis*. Also listed are *Flores Sanctorum, Speculum, Spiritalum, Auretous Angustines, de pastoribus,* a book on grammar, the *Life of Christ,* and in conclusion a primer and three volumes called digests.

V. H. St. John Hope, *On an Inventory of the goods of the Collegiate Church of the Holy Trinity, Arundel, taken 1st October 9 Henry viiij (1517).*
    Archaedogia, 2nd series, Vol. XI (1908), *cf.* R. B. K. Petch, *op. cit.,* Chap. xvj, pp. 259–275.

APPENDIX III

DUKE OF NORFOLK v. ARBUTHNOT
High Court of Justice

COMMON PLEAS DIVISION.
JUDGMENT
of the
RIGHT HON. LORD COLERIDGE, C.J.
17th May, 1879

Parol Evidence to explain Ambiguity in Antient Grant — Collegiate Church — Chancel — Dedication — Dissolution of Antient Monastic Priory — Surrender to the Crown — Re-Grant.

The monastic priory of Arundel which had long existed 'in the parochial church of Arundel' or 'of St. Nicolas Arundel', and which is said to have been founded by Roger de Montgomery (afterwards created Earl of Arundel) about the time of the Norman Conquest, was suppressed or dissolved in the reign of Richard II (about the year 1380), and a college consisting of a master or warden and twelve seculars or chaplains was by the king's licence created in its stead. The instrument of foundation contained rules or statutes for the government of the members of the college, and for the services to be celebrated 'in ecclesia prefata'.
    The church of St. Nicolas Arundel, which, architecturally considered, was one entire building all apparently of the same date, was a 'cross-church', with a nave and aisles; a central tower; transepts rather shorter than would be usual in a church of such proportions; and eastward of the central tower and transepts,

a chapel (known as the Fitzalan Chapel) occupying the place commonly filled by the parish chancel; a north aisle called the Lady Chapel; and at the north-east corner a room originally a 'sacristy', but which had for many years been used as a school-room, and as a place where the election to offices in the corporation of Arundel were habitually held.

In 1511, disputes having arisen between the college and the corporation of Arundel as to the repair of 'ye crosse-partes' or transepts, the bell-tower of the church, the bells and bell-furniture therein, they were submitted for arbitration to the then Earl of Arundel and the then Bishop of Chichester. These 'crosse-partes' were described as going from south to north 'inter chorum et navem ecclesiae': and the award of the Earl and Bishop was as follows,—The college are solely to repair the south transept, 'quae cancellus parochialis vulgariter nuncupatur'; the corporation and the parish are solely to repair the north transept and the whole of the nave and its aisles; and the expense of keeping up and repairing the bell-tower, bells, and bell-furniture is to be defrayed by the corporation and the parish on the one part, and the college on the other part, in equal moieties.

In the 26th year of Henry VIII (1544), the master or warden and chaplains of the college surrendered to the King 'totam cantariam sive collegium nostrum prædictum; ac etiam totum scitum, fundum, circuitum, ambitum, vel procinctum, ac ecclesiam campanile, et cimiterium ejusdem cantariae sive collegii, cum omnibus et omnimodis domibus, edificiis, ortis, pomariis, gardinis, terra et solo infra dictum circuitum et procinctum cantariae sive collegii praedicti', &c. And in the same year the King in almost the same identical words re-granted the college and its possessions to Henry Earl of Arundel and his heirs.

Since the surrender and re-grant of 1544 no act of religious worship had taken place or prayers said within the walls of the Fitzalan Chapel, with the exception of the reading of the Church of England burial service over some of the bodies which had been buried there,—those of members of the Duke's family who had abandoned the religion of their ancestors; and during the whole of that time the plaintiff and his predecessors had claimed to exclude and had in fact excluded the vicar and parishioners of Arundel from the whole of the disputed building. An iron lattice-work or grille filling the arch which would be commonly called the 'chancel arch', and which apparently was old as the building itself, and divided the part in dispute from the rest of the structure, was locked on the eastern side (there being no key-hole on the other side), and the key always kept by the Earls and Dukes. Vaults had been made and interments had taken place in the building, both in the Fitzalan Chapel and in the Lady Chapel, at the sole pleasure of the Dukes. No faculty had ever been applied for, no registration had taken place, nor had any fees been paid in respect of such vaults and interments. Against these acts of ownership exercised by the plaintiff's predecessors during more than three hundred years, there was not a single act of ownership proved on the part of either the vicar or the parishioners. The answers returned by successive churchwardens for a long series of years (from 1844 to 1875) to articles of visitation episcopal and archdiaconal, all shewed that they assumed the south transept to be the chancel of the parochial church, and the east end of the south transept to be the east end of the church:—

HELD, by Lord Coleridge, C.J., upon motion for judgment, that these facts were conclusive to shew that the building in question was not the chancel of the parochial church of St. Nicolas Arundel, but had always remained the private property of the Duke of Norfolk and his predecessors, and that a legal origin for such possession must be presumed; and that, even if the building in question could be shewn clearly to have been the parochial chancel in the fourteenth and fifteenth centuries, every presumption possible in point of law ought to be made in favour of a possession so exclusive, so old, and so unbroken.

Where the words of an antient grant are ambiguous or vague, and leave it doubtful what may have been the intention of the donor, recourse may be had to evidence of long and uniform user to interpret or explain them.

An aisle or a chancel under the same roof with and open to the rest of a church *may* be shewn by evidence to be the property of a private person.

Semble, that an integral portion of a church (the church being one and undivided, considered architecturally,) cannot properly be called a 'church'.

Statement of Claim

1.   The plaintiff is tenant in tail male in possession of a piece of land with the building thereon called the Fitzalan chapel, in the parish of Arundel, in the county of Sussex.

2.   On or about the 2nd July, 1877, the defendant, by himself and his servants, broke and entered the said piece of land and building of the plaintiff, and wrongfully pulled down and destroyed a certain wall therein, and divers of the bricks composing the said wall.

3.   The defendant threatens and intents to commit similar trespasses and injuries on and to the said premises, unless he is restrained by the injunction of the Court.

The plaintiff claimed £100 damages, and the costs of the action; and an injunction to restrain the defendant, his servants, agents, and workmen from further entering upon the land and building, and from doing further damage to the wall.

The statement of defence and counter-claim, so far as is material, was as follows:—

3.   Before and at the time of the alleged trespasses, the defendant was, and still is, vicar, incumbent, and officiating minister of the church of the parish of Arundel.

4.   The building mentioned in the first paragraph of the statement of claim is the great chancel or choir of the ancient church of the parish of Arundel, and the defendant, as and being such vicar, incumbent, and officiating minister as aforesaid, was and is entitled to the possession of the great chancel or choir end of the nave of the said church, and also was and is entitled to have free ingress and egress betwixt the great chancel and nave, and also to have the light and air pass without obstruction betwixt the great chancel and nave.

5.   The vicar of the said church for the time being has as such always been

possessed of the nave of the said church of the parish of Arundel, which nave has also adjoined the piece of land in the first paragraph of the statement of claim mentioned; and the defendant, as such vicar, at the time of the alleged trespasses, so possessed as aforesaid. The vicar of the said church has been accustomed to have the light and air enter into the said nave through a certain antient arch and screen, and has always been accustomed to have such access of light and air and such ingress and egress actually and without interruption from time immemorial, or for forty years, or for twenty years, or for a long time before the bringing of this action, and, except in the case of the access of light and air for such period of twenty years, such user has been of right.

6.   The user in the last paragraph mentioned establishes the defendant's right to the said access of light and air, and his right to the said ingress and egress, under 2 & 3 Wm. 4, c.71, or by prescription, or in virtue of a grant or charter now lost of which the former existence is to be presumed or inferred, or otherwise; and the defendant relies on such rights or one of them as a justification for his acts.

(There was a similar justification as 'one of the parishioners or one of the inhabitants of the said parish of Arundel'.)

10.   The plaintiff wrongfully and improperly, and without the consent or authority of the ordinary, or of the defendant, or of the parishioners or inhabitants, erected the wall mentioned in the second paragraph of the statement of claim, across the church at the part where the piece of land in the first paragraph of the statement of claim mentioned adjoins the nave, thereby completely separating the said piece of land from the nave and wrongfully obstructing and interfering with the defendant's possession of the said piece of land, as and being the great chancel and nave, and the defendant's right to free ingress and egress and the passage of light and air betwixt the said piece of land, as and being the great chancel and nave, and the passage of light and air through the said arch and screen.

11.   The defendant, because the wall so obstructed and interfered with some or one of the rights hereinbefore claimed by him, necessarily pulled down and destroyed the wall, or part thereof, doing no unnecessary damage in that behalf; which pulling down and destroying were the trespasses complained of.

The defendant claimed by way of counter-claim:—1. £100 damages in respect of the wrongful erection and continuance of the said wall by the plaintiff. 2. An injunction restraining the plaintiff from continuing the wall or so much thereof as hindered or obstructed any of the rights claimed by the defendant, and ordering the plaintiff to remove the wall or such part thereof as aforesaid, and to restore the church and the site of the wall to the condition in which they were before the plaintiff began to build the said wall.

The plaintiff in reply, set out the provision against alienation contained in an Act of 3 Car. 1, for the settlement of the family estates of the Earls and Dukes, and denied that the building in question was the great chancel or choir of the parish church as alleged, or that the defendant or the parishioners of Arundel possessed or had exercised the rights claimed therein. Issue thereon.

The case was tried before Lord Coleridge, C.J., on the 25th March, 1879, and was argued on motion for judgment on a subsequent day by Dr. Stephens,

Q.C. (with whom were C. Bowen and Dr. Walter Phillimore), for the plaintiff, and by Charles Q.C. (with whom was Jeune), for the defendant.

The contention on the part of the plaintiff was, that the building in question, the Fitzalan Chapel, at the east end of the church of St. Nicolas Arundel (in the position usually occupied by the chancel), was and always had been the sole and exclusive property of the Duke of Norfolk and his ancestors, and that the parish church of Arundel was confined to that portion of the building which constituted the south transept, with its aisles. Besides a large body of documentary evidence, all of which is fully considered and discussed in the judgment, the following authorities were referred to,—Griffin v. Dighton;[1] Rich v. Bushnell;[2] Churton v. Frewen;[3] Chapman v. Jones;[4] Kempe v. Wickes;[5] 1 Phill. Eccl. Law. 160.

On the part of the defendant it was contended that the building in question was and always had been the chancel of the parochial church of St. Nicolas Arundel; and the following authorities were cited:—Warwick v. Queen's College, Oxford;[6] Ritchings v. Cordingly;[7] Durst v. Masters;[8] Carr v. Mostyn;[9] Bright v. Walker.[10]

Cur. adv. vult.

Lord Coleridge, C.J., delivered judgment as follows:—

This is an action of trespass for breaking down a wall built on the plaintiff's land. The defendant is the vicar of the parish of Arundel; and he pleads, in substance, that the wall was built so as to obstruct his right of entrance into the chancel of his church, and to prevent the passage of light and air from the chancel to the church, and that he broke down the wall because it obstructed and interfered with his rights. The case was tried before me without a jury, and I reserved my judgment on the conclusion of the hearing, rather because of its interest and importance than that I had any serious doubt as to the view which it is now my duty to express.

Its interest and importance, however, are rather in the past than for the future; and arise chiefly out of the ancient institutions and great historical families of which during the evidence and the arguments we heard so much. The principles of decision are simple and familiar; and, whether I apply them rightly or wrongly can be of little consequence except to the parties to this particular proceeding; for, the facts of this case are, as far as I know, peculiar. Neither my own limited knowledge nor the far wider learning and research of the able counsel engaged in the argument have furnished me with my case exactly in point, or even with one in which the circumstances are so far analogous as to afford me either an authority or a guide. I have also received many communications since the hearing of the case from a great variety of persons, which I have not sent to the parties in the action before me, only because they had no real bearing upon the case, being no more than statements of what the writers supposed to be the legal rights of persons in respect of other chapels in other churches under other circumstances. I did, indeed, at the close of the hearing invite, not further argument, but further information on one definite point, viz. whether an integral portion of any church (the church being one and undivided, considered architecturally,) had ever itself been called in any authentic legal or historical document, not chancel, or chapel, or chantry, or choir, or aisle, but *church*. It was perhaps unwise to invite any communication after the close of a full and deliberate argument; but, though I have received various papers, they have none of them been confined to this definite point, nor has any one conveyed to me the information I desired. It was not a matter decisive of the case, though it leaves the interpretation of one interesting document conjectural or doubtful. I proceed to state what I conceive to be the fair effect of the documents and facts proved before me; and, if these are accurately set forth, the conclusion almost inevitably follows.

It is not very clear what were the relations between the parish of Arundel and the small monastic body which at the time of the Norman Conquest or very soon after that event was undoubtedly established there; nor, except as matter of antiquarian curiosity, is it at all important to ascertain them. It is indeed clear that they were rectors of the parish and performed the sacred offices in the parish church of Arundel then as now dedicated to St. Nicolas. But the real history of the case begins with the foundation of the College of Arundel by Richard Earl of Arundel and Surrey in the third year of Richard II, A.D. 1379 or 1380. I mention, to shew that I have not forgotten, but I do not think it the least necessary here to comment in detail upon the inquisition of the 3rd Richard II, which forewent the licence of the King. The licence of the King to the Earl for the foundation, the instrument by which the Earl founded, and the statutes by which he ordered the government of college, are all preserved. The licence is in Dugdale, the other documents are preserved in the registry at Chichester, and have been produced before me. The monastic priory was suppressed, dissolved, or annulled (adnullare and adnullatio are the words used); at any rate, it ceased to exist; and a college consisting of twelve seculars called chaplains and a master or warden was created in its stead. Both in the royal licence and in the instrument of foundation the priory is said to have existed 'in the parochial church of Arundel',[11] and 'in the parochial church of St. Nicolas Arundel'.[12] The Earl is empowered by the licence to give a name to the *College*; and, when he founds it, he says it is to be 'ad honorem Omnipotentis Trinitatis, Patris, Filii, et Spiritus Sancti, ipsius Ecclesiae jam *partoni*, Gloriosae Virginis Mariae omniumque sanctorum'. The 7th chapter of the statutes,— it being recited that the College 'in Ecclesia praedicta' (i.e. the parish church of St. Nicolas) 'ad augmentationem Divini cultus pro noto sit astrictum',— goes on to enact that the members of the college are to reside 'in ipso collegio', and are never to absent themselves 'a quibuscunque officiis Divinis in *ea ecclesia* observandis'. It enacts further in great detail the duties of the members in respect of the divine offices, so that the offices 'in ecclesia praefata provisius et honorificentius celebrentur'; and, further, that none of the members of the college shall go to perform service 'ad ecclesias convicinas', manifestly neighbouring parish churches, except in certain cases specified in the statute. The 8th chapter makes provision for the celebration of divers masses,—one, 'magna missa', 'in magno altari', another, 'missa de Gloriosa Virgine', 'ad summum altare' till a special altar for the Virgin shall be provided —and other masses all to be celebrated 'in dicta' or in eadem ecclesia'. It is also provided that on certain occasions, 'post magnam missam in *cancello* celebratam', certain psalms and prayers shall be recited in the *choir*,—'chancel' and 'choir' being used apparently as synonymes. And, further, that certain masses shall be celebrated 'ad diversa altaria' so that the parishioners 'dictae ecclesiae' and others may hear them. So far is the language of these documents.

It appears further that the whole fabric as it stands now is of substantially the same date, and was probably all built continuously, with no break between the building of one portion and another, at the close of the 14th or the very beginning of the 15th century. It appears also that the iron lattice-work or grille filling the arch which would be commonly called the chancel arch, is as old as the building, and that the lock and key in it are of the same date.

It may be convenient shortly to state that the church, regarded as one building, is a cross church, with a nave and aisles; a central tower; transepts rather shorter than would be usual in a church of such proportions; and, east-ward of the central tower and transepts, the disputed building consisting of a long and beautifully proportioned chapel occupying the place commonly filled by the parish chancel; a north aisle called, and no doubt rightly called, the Lady Chapel; and at the north-east corner a room probably originally used as a sacristy, now disused, but which, as will appear in more detail by-and-bye, was for many years used as a school-room, and as the place where the elections to the office of mayor certainly, and I think to other offices in the corporation of Arundel, habitually were held.

I am of opinion that the church spoken of in these documents is the whole parish church of St. Nicolas Arundel, including what is now used by the parish, and what is claimed by the Duke of Norfolk. Speaking only, as only I can speak, as a man of ordinary education and experience, I cannot help knowing that there are numerous instances in different parts of England of churches still called collegiate, which were before the Reformation the churches of colleges of secular priests, which were also the churches of parishes of which these colleges were rectors, the freeholds of which churches were in the colleges in the sense in which the freehold of any church is in an ordinary ecclesiastical rector, and in which the parishioners had certain rights and the colleges had certain other rights,—rights co-existing and not conflicting; which churches were nevertheless one not two, and that not merely architecturally and to the eye, but really and in law.

We shall see as we go on whether the documents shew that in after time it was different; but, at and soon after the foundation of the college, I do not at all doubt that, if it had been asked what was the parish church of Arundel, the present church of St. Nicolas in its architectural integrity would have been pointed out; and, if it had been asked what was the church of the college of the Holy Trinity of Arundel, the questioner would have been shewn the very same building in its architectural integrity; yet, as the grille shews, the college practically had the exclusive use of the part eastward of it, the parishioners as a rule had the use only of the nave with its aisles and transepts. It may be that as we were told by a very great and learned architect, the pulpit in the nave, and the high altar in the extreme east end of the church, which was in view from the pulpit, were, as he phrased it, 'worked together'; meaning, I suppose, that, as the preacher could see the high altar, he might, and perhaps did, direct the attention of his hearers to it and to the sacred elements upon it. But the existence of the iron-work filling the whole arch, a circumstance admitted to be most unusual, seems to me to shew that there may have been a reservation to the college and to its members only of that part of the church which was eastward of the iron-work. That the Earl of Arundel who founded the college and built the church might, if he pleased, so distribute his gift between the college and parishioners is, I think quite clear. There is nothing in the documents I have examined to shew that he did not. Is there anything in those which follow? Certainly not, in my opinion, in the will or wills of Earl Thomas, executed in 30 Hen. 5, A.D. 1415, not many years after the foundation of the college and the building of the church. He desires to be buried 'in our *college* of Arundel before the high altar'; and, again, 'in the choir of the *college* of the Holy Trinity of Arundel'. Neither of these expressions appears to me to mean, not to be even capable of meaning, that the building now claimed by the Duke of Norfolk *was* the college, which certainly was *not* either in 1415 or at any other time; both of them appear to me to imply that, in 1415, this building was a part of the college in the sense that either it belonged to the college or was at least a building in which the college had peculiar and perhaps exclusive rights.

I do not think that anything is to be gathered from the admissions by the Bishops of Chichester to the vicarage of Arundel and to the mastership of the college of Arundel, several of which to each office between the years 1405 and 1528 have been put in evidence. They shew that there was besides the rectory a vicarage of Arundel, to which the college presented and the bishop instituted, sometimes a member of the college and sometimes not. But this shews nothing, and the instrument by which the vicarage was created, and which might possibly have shewn something, does not exist, or at any rate has not been produced.

But there is a document of 1511 to which both sides have appealed,— the Duke as shewing that at that date the building he now claims belonged absolutely to the college and that the parish had no rights therein,—the vicar of Arundel as shewing that this building was then really the great chancel of Arundel church; and he thence contends that, if this was so in 1511, nothing has since happened to deprive it of its character. The document is curious. It appears that in 1511 there had been disputes between the college and the corporation and parish of Arundel as to the repair of 'ye crosse partes', or, as we should now say, the transepts, the bell-tower of the church, and the bells and bell-furniture therein; and that all parties had agreed to submit the matters for arbitration to the then Earl of Arundel and the then Bishop of Chichester. These 'crosse partes' are described as going from south to north 'inter chorum et navem ecclesiae'; and the award of the Earl and Bishop was as follows: The college are solely to repair the south transept, 'quae cancellus parochialis vulgariter nuncupatur'; the corporation and the parish are solely to repair the north transept and the whole of the nave and its aisles; and the expense of keeping up and repairing the bell-tower, bells, and bell-furniture is to be defrayed by the corporation and parish on the one part and the college on the other part in equal moieties. I do not notice the temporary provision as to the key, as it applies to the bell-tower only.

Such is the effect of this document; and it appears to me to make out with tolerable certainty several propositions. First, that in 1511 the whole building was commonly spoken of as one church. Next, that the parish did at that time in fact use the south transept as their chancel, and that the south transept was commonly called the parish chancel. Next, that at that time in fact the building now in dispute was not *used* as a chancel by the parish, and that the high altar of the parish was not then there. Next, that the college were charged with the repair of the parish chancel as well as with that of the disputed building and of the Lady Chapel, because, being rectors, it was equitable that they should repair what was in fact the chancel of the parish. Next, that, the nave and aisles and north transept being in fact the portion of the entire church used by the parish other than their own chancel, it was fair that the parish should repair them. Lastly, that, the bell-tower and the bells therein being used alike for the college services and for the parish services, the college should bear half of that expense the whole of which in ordinary cases would have been borne by the parish. Such appears to me to be the evidence of fact supplied by the award; and I think it is strong evidence to shew that the distribution of the building between the college and the parish which might have been made by the Earl who founded the college and built the church, was made by him in fact and was existing in practice some 130 years after his foundation.

Then we come to the surrender of the college to Henry VIII., and the re-grant by Henry to the Earl of Arundel of that date. These are interesting documents apart from their bearing on the case; for, the ecclesiastical Latin in which the surrender is written appears almost unable to express the absolute willingness and eager self-sacrifice with which the members of the college stripped themselves of all they possessed, and reduced themselves to beggary, without any pressure whatever from their most illustrious and invincible prince and lord Henry VIII. Recent history teaches us to believe implicitly the absolute truth of such statements in such documents from such persons at such a time; and no statements certainly can be stronger. The master or warden and the fellows of the college or chantry of the Holy Trinity of and in Arundel surrender to the King 'totam cantariam sive collegium nostrum praedictum; ac etiam totum scitum, fundum, circuitum, ambitum vel procinctum, ac ecclesiam campanile et cimiterium ejusdem cantariae sive collegii, cum omnibus et omnimodus domibus, edificiis, ortis, pomariis, gardinis, terra et solo infradictum circuitum et procinctum cantariae sive collegii praedicti'. They then surrender their whole property real and personal to the sole use of the King, his heirs, successors, and assigns; and at the conclusion of the document they warrant and assure to the King, inter alia, 'dictam cantariam sive collegium nostrum, ac etiam totum scitum, fundum, circuitum, ambitum, et procinctum, mansionem et ecclesiam nostram praedictam, ac omnia et singula maneria', and so forth.

Much reliance was placed by the counsel for the defendant upon the word *ecclesia* in the beginning and end of this surrender, as shewing that the college surrendered to the King the disputed building only; for that, as the parish church did not belong to them, they could not surrender it. But they had a certain property in the parish church, as they had in the churchyard, and what they had they surrendered. They had other rectories and benefices belonging to them in the counties of Sussex and Southampton, and these they speak of and surrender as 'ecclesias nostras praedictas', in the plural, shewing that they used 'church' in its popular and ordinary sense, and that, where they possessed an advowson or a presentation, they spoke of the church connected with such advowson or presentation as their church. I think there is no ground whatever from the language of this surrender for contending that at the date of it the architectural whole of the parish church of Arundel was divided into two churches; and that under the term 'ecclesia' only the building now in dispute was intended to be or was in fact surrendered.

I pass to the re-grant of the college and its possessions (together with other properties) by the King to the Earl of Arundel in the same year as the surrender. The King grants to the Earl 'totum scitum, fundum, ambitum, circuitum, et procinctum nuper ecclesiae collegiatae sive collegii Sanctae Trinitatis de Arundel in comitatu nostro Sussexiae; alias dictae nuper collegii sive cantariae Sanctae Trinitatis de vel in Arundel in comitatu nostro Sussexiae modo dissolutae. Ac ecclesiam campanile et cimiterium ejusdem nuper collegii sive cantariae. Ac etiam omnia et singula messuagia, domos, infra scitum, ambitum, circuitum, et procinctum dictae nuper ecclesiae collegiatae collegii sive cantariae praedictae existentes aut dictae nuper ecclesiae collegiatae collegio sive cantariae aliquo modo dudum spectantes sive pertinentes; ac parcellum possessionum et reventionum ejusdem ecclesiae collegiatae collegii sive cantariae dudum existentes'. I have set out this somewhat long passage in detail to shew that in this document collegiate church, college, and chantry, are used over and over again as simple synonymes. They are used in a precisely similar collocation at least a dozen times more in the course of the grant, and always in a like sense.

It was argued, as I understood, that in the grant the word 'ecclesia' in connection with campanile et cimiterium might mean, and that in truth they did mean, the building now in dispute, and not the whole church in its architectural integrity. But I think the argument untenable. The King is careful (see p. 6 of the printed grant) to grant to the Earl only what the college surrendered to him, professes to grant no right or estate in the granted premises except the right or estate of the college.

I have said already that the college did in my judgment grant the whole church to the King, i.e. according to their estate and right in it, as part of their property; and I have given my reasons for so thinking. If therefore the college granted it in any sense to the King, in that sense the King granted it to the Earl. The language also fairly considered appears to me to lead to the same result. The church of the *college* I could understand being at least possibly the disputed building; but the church of the collegiate *church*, the church of the *chantry*, must mean in my judgment the church of the corporate body called by these various names, i.e. the church of which the advowson was in them, the freehold of which and of the church-yard was in them, i.e. the whole undivided church of St. Nicolas Arundel, in which the college and the parish had the respective rights which I have already indicated. The grant of the bells and lead, amongst a variety of other goods and chattels, makes no difference; and I mention it lest I should be thought to have overlooked it.

The estates of the Earl of Arundel, and amongst them what had been granted by Henry VIII., became forfeited to the Crown by the attainder of the then Earl in the reign of Elizabeth. They were re-granted to Thomas Earl of Arundel by James I., in the second year of his reign. There is nothing in the language of the grant of James I. which calls for observa-tion. In the third year of Charles I. a private Act of Parliament settled certain estates inalienably upon the then Earl of Arundel and his heirs, and, in default of heirs male, upon Lord William Howard and his heirs male,—the present heir male being the Duke of Norfolk, the plaintiff. The value of this Act is only as a piece of evidence respecting the names which certain things bore at the time when it was passed; for, it grants nothing; it only settles and assures what was already the Earl's. But it is to be observed that it treats as property and as subjects of settlement things the property in which and the rights in respect of which were of very various sorts. It settles, for instance, the borough of Arundel, the manor of Arundel, the rectorie of Arundel, the forest of Arundel, the college house called the college of Arundel, the almshouse of Arundel, with a great multitude of other things, each, it is to be assumed, according to the estate and interest which the Earl of Arundel then had in them respec-tively. A sum of 210 l. a year is reserved out of certain properties, to be paid to the Fishmongers' Company in London, to be by them expended in repairing 'the castle of Arundel and the chapel adjoining to the church of Arundel wherein some of the Earls of Arundel lye buried'; and some reliance was placed in argument upon these last words. But they are, after all, a description only in a private Act of Parliament; and though I do not at all doubt that they describe the building now in dispute, they do not by themselves shew its legal relation to the church, still less do they ascertain whether this chapel was then used as a chancel, as it might have been or whether it was then as it had been for many years practically separated off from the rest of the building. And no evidence was given before me, either from the Fishmongers' Company or otherwise, to shew that the sum mentioned in the Act of Charles had been or was still paid to the company, or on what part of the whole fabric, if on any part, the money had been or was expended by the company if they received it.

This ends what may be called the documentary title to this building. There is no language in my opinion in any part of it conclusive either for the plaintiff or the defendant. The founder may have intended to grant to the college the exclusive use of so much of the church as lay eastwards of the transept. His language is at least patient of such an interpretation; and the award of the Bishop and the Earl in 1511 is at least some, I think myself it is strong, evidence to shew that the usage of many years had at that time so interpreted it. Whatever the college had from the founder passed from Henry VIII. to the Earl of Arundel, and from Henry Earl of Arundel to the Duke of Norfolk. If the words of grants are ambiguous or vague (I say, if they are so, because in my opinion the words here are plain enough), it is common law and common sense to have recourse to the evidence of fact to explain them. What have been in fact the rights enjoyed ever since the Reformation in respect of this building by the Earls of Arundel and their successors the Dukes of Norfolk? The answer must be, the most absolute rights of ownership which, regard being had to be nature of the property, were ever proved in a Court of Justice. I confess that, when I saw to try this cause, knowing nothing about it but what the pleadings disclosed, and having passed a day at Arundel endeavouring to get into my mind a clear view of the buildings and of their surroundings, I fully expected that there would be disputed or conflicting facts, that at the least there would be some things proved which would call upon the plaintiff for careful explanation. But there is scarcely a fact proved by the plaintiff which has been disputed; scarcely anything which can be called a fact proved on the part of the defendant.

I proceed to state some facts of ownership, most of them undisputed, all established before me by the clearest proof. Since the surrender of the college to the King in 1544, no act of religious worship has taken place within the walls of the disputed building, with the exception of the reading of the Church of England burial service over some of the bodies which have been interred therein,—an exception which I will separately notice. No prayers have been said; no Holy Communion has been administered. During the whole of that time the plaintiff and his predecessors have claimed to exclude and have in fact excluded the vicar and the parishioners from the whole of the disputed building. The iron lattice-work was locked on the eastern side, and the Earls or Dukes have kept the key. In the fact that the lock was on the eastern side there is nothing: out it is quite otherwise as to the custody of the key. There are other entrances to it, and of those likewise the keys have been kept in the same custody. In 1858, the key, not of the lattice-work, but of a door, was lent by the then Duke to the then vicar; but after a while it was reclaimed by the Duke and returned by the vicar. Vaults have been made and interments have taken place in the building, both in that part of it which has been called the Fitzalan Chapel, and in that part which no doubt was the Lady Chapel, at the sole pleasure of the Dukes. No faculty has been applied for, no registration has taken place, no fees have been paid in respect of such vaults and such interments. Further, the Dukes have at their pleasure disinterred bodies in this building, and have changed the places of their sepulture, without any faculty being obtained for the purpose.

These are acts done by the predecessors of the plaintiff, and done during more than three hundred years, with nothing to set against them. The utter neglect of this beautiful and interesting building by the same line of owners is almost equal proof of the absolute character of their ownership. It is, no doubt, the privilege of an owner to let his property fall into decay; a privilege of which former Dukes of Norfolk have availed themselves in respect of this building to the utmost extent. A hundred years ago, as a print of that date shews, there was a rich carved roof which, whether it was removed or fell down, at any rate no longer exists. There are costly and noble monuments of the Fitzalans, amongst them a singularly rich and splendid alabaster altar tomb with two recumbent figures on it, all in a state of dirt, neglect, and mutilation, which families far less illustrious than those of Howard and Fitzalan seldom allow to exist in the monuments of their ancestors. It was proved also that the building had been used as a lumber-room and as a workshop; and that the access to it which was denied to the vicar and parishioners, was freely granted to the owls and bats. There may have been reasons why this state of squalor and ruin was permitted, of the weight of which I am no judge, for I do not know them; but, certainly, a stronger assertion of an absolute right of property in a patron of an ecclesiastical building than to exclude every one from it, to treat it as a store-place for tools and ladders, and to suffer it to become almost a ruin, can hardly be conceived.

It is quite true that from time to time members of the family of the Dukes of Norfolk have been buried in the disputed building, whose burials are registered, or who appear to have been buried with the rites of the Church of England; and that in these latter cases the body has been borne into it from the nave of the church through the iron lattice-work and the service said there by the vicar or some English clergyman representing him. The registers from 1691 to the present day contain the registry of sixteen burials of the Norfolk family; and of these seven appear to have taken place with Church of England rites, the earliest of this latter class, at least so far as the registers afford evidence on the subject, in 1824. But, first, this has been the exception, not the rule; and, whereas the rule is very difficult to explain, except upon the view of the case represented by the Duke; the exceptions are readily capable of an explanation, which renders them of little weight in favour of that presented by the vicar. Every time that the Duke buried without service, or built a vault, or removed bodies in this building,—especially since 1847, when the church of Arundel was closed against burials by Order in Council,—he was, unless the building belonged to him, breaking the law and defying ecclesiastical authority. But, as to the burials within it with Church of England rites, some of the bodies may have been those of Protestants (for, there have been Protestants in the Howard family) or of Roman Catholics either who had had no objection in their lives, or as to whom their kinsmen had no objection after death, that the Church of England service should be read over their remains. This state of feeling is in fact not uncommon in the old Roman Catholic families in England; and the fact, therefore, that such burials as I have mentioned have taken place, though proper to be noticed, cannot countervail the weight which attaches to the length and prevalence of the contrary practice.

While such has been the assertion of property in respect of this building for more than three hundred years on the part of the Duke and his predecessors, and such the user to which they can point in support of the legality of what they assert, what has been the conduct on the part of the vicar and parishioners? Absolute acquiescence is an expression hardly strong enough to be applied to it. This, indeed, there has been. No vicar has asserted any right; no bishop or archdeacon has attempted to exercise any authority; no churchwardens or parishioners have ever made any claim, till a very few years ago, in respect of this building. But this is by no means all. Articles of visitation both episcopal and archidiaconal have been put in before me, ranging from 1844 to 1875. In these articles questions are asked as to the state of repair of the church *as well the chancel* as the body thereof'. The answers are 'good', 'very good', 'excellent'; and this at a time when the utter squalor and total disrepair of what is now claimed as chancel was notorious and has been proved. Questions are asked as to the existence of the Tables of the Ten Commandments *at the east end of the church according to the canon*'. The answers are, that they exist, that they are in excellent order; in one instance 'quite a pattern' is the parochial language. This at a time when according to the present contention the east end of the church was ruinous, and there were no commandments on it according to the canon. In more than one instance, they are expressly said to be in *the chancel*. All these answers shew conclusively that the vicar and churchwardens treated the south transept as the chancel; and that, if they ever heard of, they expressly abstained from giving any countenance to, the contention of the present defendant.

In two instances alone is there some trace to be found of the present contention. In 1850, the churchwardens state, in answer to the question as to the state of repair of the church and chancel, that the church is in good repair, 'but we have nothing to do with the chancel'. In 1865, the churchwardens at first state that the chancel as well as the body of the church is in very good repair: but, as to the Ten Commandments, they say that they are 'set up in the chancel (so called) over the Communion Table, but the chancel proper has been usurped by the Duke of Norfolk'; and, in answer to the question whether there have been interments recently within the walls of the church, they say, 'No: the *last* interment was in the chancel claimed by the Duke of Norfolk now as private property'. These answers are signed by Mr. Holmes, a highly respectable and intelligent solicitor, who was a witness before me, and who appears to have been one of the churchwardens of Arundel for a great many years. But this is the only instance in which this claim appears while he was churchwarden. Both before and *after* 1865, he signs answers in the ordinary form, which assume the south transept to be the chancel of the church, and the east wall of the south transept to be the east end of the church. He said indeed, that he signed these answers without much thought; but that can hardly be so as to the answers of 1865; and, as to the others, I must observe that they do not all follow one form of words, that the language of them is occasionally individual and characteristic, and that, if it were otherwise, those who sign formal and important documents of this kind cannot escape from the fair effect of their language by saying that they used it carelessly; and, further, that, if the claim now put forward had been persistently made in the answers to these articles, I should undoubtedly have heard much as to the great weight to be given to these answers from the learned and able counsel for the defendant. The answers which I have noticed in 1850 and 1865 do indeed show that at those dates some of the parishioners at least held opinions in favour of the claim now put forward by the vicar; but, as nothing was done, at the furthest and the utmost they shew no more. I have had no articles proved before me of an earlier date than 1844; but, as far as they go, and making due allowance for the two exceptions I have noticed, the weight of evidence to be deduced from them is entirely in favour of the Duke and against the vicar and the parish. If, therefore, I felt bound to say, as I did, that the evidence of the acts done by the Duke's predecessors was almost as strong as evidence could be in favour of the plaintiff, I am bound to say further that the evidence afforded thus far by the conduct of former vicars and parishioners is almost as strong as evidence can be against the defendant.

There is a transaction of the year 1848, between the Duke of Norfolk and the corporation of Arundel which, and the building in relation to which it took place, it is necessary to notice. At the north-east end of the Lady Chapel there is a small building connected internally by an ancient passage with the Lady Chapel, which it seems agreed was used before the Reformation as a sacristy. Down to the year 1848, at least to within twenty years of that date, but *from* what point of time was left uncertain, it was shewn to have been used as a school-room, and as the place where elections to offices in the corporation of Arundel had annually been held. In or about 1848, the Duke had turned a road, had given a piece of ground to the churchyard, and had built at considerable expense the present Town Hall of Arundel; and by a mutual conveyance in 1848, the Duke conveys certain premises to the corporation, and the corporation, 'as far as they lawfully or equitably can or may, convey to the Duke, inter alia, the old school or court house and the site thereof'. I do not myself think this transaction of any great importance. It is barely thirty years ago. The cautious and hesitating language of the deed seems to shew great doubt on the part of those who advised the corporation whether the corporation had any such right or property to convey, and whether, if it had, it could now by such an instrument convey it. As far as it goes, however, the inference to be gathered from the transaction is in favour of the plaintiff. No one except the corporation appears to have claimed any right in this building against the Duke; and if it did belong to the corporation, then it is another instance of an integral part of an ecclesiastical building having in times long beyond living memory become the property of laymen, and having been used for purposes wholly secular and entirely alien from those to which in the time of the college it had in all likelihood been devoted.

Why should I hesitate to give its natural effect to evidence such as I have described? It has been argued that the Dukes of Norfolk were great and powerful noblemen, and that, as the vicar and parishioners of Arundel had no power to contest their usurpations; so acquiescence in these usurpations is not to be used as evidence of their legal origin. I do not know that, as judge of law, or as in this case of fact, I can, or that if I can I ought so to deal with such evidence as this. But the argument, whatever it may be worth, is I think completely met by the fact that, if the Howards were a powerful family, as in one sense no doubt they were, also a family belonging, not indeed exclusively, but on the whole and generally, to a religion for many long years proscribed and persecuted. Their ecclesiastical patronage, if Roman Catholics, was exercised by the Universities; they were, if Roman Catholics, the objects of a penal legislation which is to be found described in the burning words of Mr. Burke,[13] and which I take the freedom to say was a disgrace to a civilized country; and I cannot and do not believe in fact that if this building had belonged to the parish of Arundel, there would have been no attempt on the part of any vicar or parishioners to revindicate it, none on the part of any Bishop of Chichester or Archdeacon to exercise any authority within it, claimed and held as it was by Roman Catholics during so many years of the centuries which rolled by from the time of Queen Elizabeth to the time of George IV.

I felt some difficulty from the fact that the Lady Chapel appears to have been treated exactly on the same footing, and to have been as exclusively as the building called the Fitzalan Chapel in the possession of the plaintiff and his predecessors in title, at least from the time of the Reformation. It is, as far as my knowledge of such matters extends, more difficult to suppose that the Lady Chapel was not originally open to the use of the whole parish, than under the circumstances of this particular case it is as to the rest of the building in dispute. But the alleged trespass here committed was not on any part of the Lady Chapel and, except indirectly, no question arises as to the Lady Chapel itself regarded as a separate building. Further the evidence as to user is wholly indistinguishable as to its effect, and includes the Lady Chapel as well as the rest of the building. And, further, I observe that, in the award of 1511, it seems to be assumed that the college is to repair the Lady Chapel as well as the rest of the disputed building; which is some, indeed is strong evidence to shew that at that time the college had the exclusive use of the Lady Chapel, and that the parishioners of Arundel had then no rights therein. I come to the conclusion, therefore, that, in this case, any facts proved as to the Lady Chapel, are by no means inconsistent with the claim of the plaintiff.

It is said, however, as I understand the defendant's argument, that, in an ecclesiastical building one and entire, as this is, it is almost impossible to suppose that there would not be one and the same organization throughout it, one and the same set of rights exercised over all its parts. The nave at Carlisle, the south transept at Chester, the Lady Chapel at Ely, the crypt (I believe) at Canterbury (but on this I speak without certain knowledge), the transepts at Merton College, Oxford, are instances in which parts of a physically united building, are used by different bodies with different rights. It may be that at Wymondham, at Dunster, and in several places to which I have been referred in the very able paper of Mr. Freeman, a state of things more or less analogous to the state of things at Arundel is to be found. I do not, however, go into, for, I do not know the circumstances of, any one of these cases. Probably they differ in each case, and give rise in each case to different considerations. Probably a man better informed than myself in these matters could largely multiply the examples. In each case it is a question of evidence; and in this case it appears to me that the evidence shews that the vicar and parishioners of Arundel never had any rights in what they now claim as their chancel.

That an aisle or a chancel under the same roof with and open to the rest of a church *may* be shewn by evidence to be the property of a private person, is too clear for argument. Such cases exist in considerable numbers in all parts of England. Few of us but are aware of instances which establish this fact. That there is no legal principle to prevent it, is determined by the cases of Churton v. Frewen[14] and Chapman v. Jones.[15] The judgment of V.-C. Kindersley in the one case, and the argument of Dr. Stephens in the other, are indexes to the display of various learning upon the subject in which any one who thinks fit may indulge. I think it enough to say that the cases I have cited establish the proposition for which I have cited them; and, although it is true that the chancels or chapels which were the subjects of decision in those cases were not direct continuations of the nave, it is obvious that except as matter of evidence this can make no difference in the principle. It may be more unusual, and therefore more difficult to establish in fact that a chapel or chancel in the position of this building was not the parochial chancel of a church, and was a private chapel. But, once establish the proposition that a chapel or a chancel may be private property, and the question whether this or that building is private property in fact becomes a question of proof. I am of opinion that the proof of this building being always private property is as strong as the nature of the case allows.

I do not refer to text-books or to cases for the proposition that with evidence of the fact of possession such as exists here, a legal origin for such possession, if a legal origin is possible, is to be presumed. If an authority is needed, Jenkins v. Harvey,[16] which was tried twice, is sufficient to refer to. I content myself with saying that, if the evidence of exclusive user in this case is insufficient to establish the right of property in the plaintiff, the defendant must get a declaration that it is so from the Court of Appeal.

It is argued, indeed, that, if a place is once a parochial chancel, it always remains so; that there can be no prescription against the public;

and that the evidence of 350 years is to go for nothing. In the sense in which and for the purpose for which this proposition was pressed upon me, I doubt its truth. I apprehend that, even this building could be shewn clearly to have been the parochial chancel in the 14th and 15th centuries, every presumption possible in point of law ought to be made in favour of a possession so exclusive, so old, and so unbroken as the possession in the present case. But I need not stay to discuss the question. Here, the presumption fails. I am myself convinced and I think all the evidence shews that this building never was the parochial chancel, and the possession of the 17th, 18th and 19th centuries was but the continuation of the possession of the 14th and 15th. In truth there is nothing on the other side but the architectural evidence of a great and learned artist. There is no reason why I should hesitate to say that, if an opinion were proof of fact, there is no opinion in England to which I should listen with more respect and deference than the opinion of Mr. Butterfield. But I must determine this case to the best of my ability by proof of facts; and all the facts are, not merely according to technical rules of law but according to sense, against his opinion. Externally, and as an affair of building, any one who looks at Arundel church would, simply from what meets his eye, come to the same conclusion as Mr. Butterfield. It does not need his great authority to say that the general look of the building is in favour of the defendant. In truth his evidence was, as might be expected, a highly intelligent exposition of the architectural reasons for arriving, from the view of the building, at the conclusion at which, the view only, everyone would arrive. His evidence as to the facts of the building is unquestionable, but not really very important; when we follow him into the regions of opinion, the documents and the user of centuries appear to me to part company with him. Upon the first and most important question, therefore, —the property in the disputed building,—I am of opinion that the plaintiff has made out his case, and is entitled to my judgment.

The second question, i.e. whether the nave of the church is entitled to light and air through the arch which leads into the eastward chapel, need not detain us long. It occupies, no doubt, a large space in the pleadings, but to the defendant at least it is manifestly unimportant: If the vicar and parishioners of Arundel have no rights eastwards of the transepts, whether they have a physical division between their church and the Duke of Norfolk's chapel cannot much signify. I must however, decide this question, as it is raised; and I must decide it for the plaintiff.

The defendant justifies the trespass he has committed, by pleading that the plaintiff had by building a wall obstructed the light and air to which he on the part of his parish had a right, and that therefore he broke the wall down. But, in the first place, the very foundation of such a defence is wanting here. Assuming for his purpose, that light and air did come from the Duke of Norfolk's chapel to Arundel church, there is no evidence whatever that any sensible or serious diminution of either has been occasioned by the building of the wall which has been knocked down by the defendant. But, further, from 1811, or at latest from 1816, the parish had filled up the arch with boards on the western side of the iron lattice-work, which effectually shut out all light and air from the church, except what might come from a door at the bottom of the arch, which was proved before me to have been occasionally opened in hot weather. An attempt was made to shew that there had been an opening in the boards higher up in the arch; but the attempt failed, and there was no proof of this. In 1872 the church was restored, under a faculty, by Sir Gilbert Scott. He placed an altar and reredos right across the space where this door had been, and therefore, if the old state of things had remained, no light and scarcely any air could have come through this archway. I do not mean to decide whether this was or was not evidence of abandonment by the defendant of the rights which he now claims. But it is at any rate the strongest possible evidence that the rights were worthless, and that, if they have been interfered with in fact, it has not been to any extent which would give a legal ground of action.

It further appears to me that the 3rd and 4th sections of the Prescription Act, 2 & 3 Wm. 4, C. 71, are fatal to the maintenance of the action on this latter ground. The wall was erected by the plaintiff in September, 1873; the trespass committed by the defendant was in July, 1877. It appears from the correspondence, that, from the beginning, the Duke made the claim which he now makes; that he declined negotiation, and stood upon his rights; and that, if the vicar intended resistance, he at any rate did nothing whatever on which the Duke could bring an action for nearly four years after the wall was built. If ever, therefore, there was a right, which I gravely doubt, it has never been interfered with so as to give ground to an action, and, if it has been, the interference has been acquiesced in so as to destroy the right of action, if ever it existed. Indeed, I cannot but regret that the correspondence began with an assertion by the vicar of right to this building, which, whether so intended or not, could be met only by a counter-assertion of right on the part of the Duke. It was unwise, because it was unnecessary, to throw down the gage of battle; but, having thrown it down, it was matter of course that it should be taken up. If a man is told that he and his ancestors for centuries have been holding property which belongs to another, he must, unless he is prepared at once to yield to the claim, decline all discussion which proceed on such a basis. With the evidence now before me, I cannot wonder that the Duke of Norfolk did decline all such discussion. Possibly, I do not know, but at least possibly, if he had been approached in a different spirit, the result to the vicar and the parish might have been very different. Possibly, even now, as this contest has been conducted, though with no concession on either side, yet with courtesy on both,—possibly some solution might be arrived at which, while preserving for the Duke of Norfolk all the rights in this building which he would care to preserve, might obtain for the parish all such of it as would be of any benefit to them. I have no right, indeed, to mediate between the parties; but I have not, I think, gone beyond the duty of my office in suggesting that arrangement is possible, and, if possible, that it is on every account desirable.

Now, however, the parties are before me standing on their legal rights; and in this state of things, and for the reasons which I have set forth, I give judgment for the plaintiff for 40s. damages, and costs; and I award an injunction, as prayed for in the statement of claim. It follows that I give judgment against the defendant on his statement of defence and counter-claim, and upon the injunction he prays for therein.

Judgment accordingly.

Postscript

Notice of appeal against this judgment was duly given and the appeal was heard by the Lords Justices Bramwell, Baggallay and Brett.

Mr. Charles, Q.C., Mr. Jeue, and Mr. V. Gibbs appeared for Mr. Arbuthnot, while Sir John Holker, Q.C., and Dr. Phillimore, were retained for the Duke of Norfolk.

The appeal was heard on Monday 31 May, and after hearing the arguments of Mr. Arbuthnot's counsel for four days their Lordships gave judgment unanimously for the Duke of Norfolk without even calling on his counsel.

Notes

Crown copyright: deposited at P.R.O.

1. 5B & S. 93, 108.
2. 4 Hagg. 170.
3. Law Rep. 2 Eq. 634.
4. Law Rep. 4 Ex. 273.
5. 3 Phill. 264, 295.
6. Law Rep. 10 Eq. 105 6 Ch. App. 815.
7. 3 A. & E. 113.
8. 1 P.D. 373.
9. 5 Exch. 69.
10. 1 C.M.R. 211.
11. Deed of foundation.
12 Royal licence.
13. Speech at the Bristol election in 1780; 3 Burke's Works, 423, 424.
14. Law Rep. 2 Eq. 634.
15. 1 C.M. & R. 877; 2 C.M. & R. 393.
16. Law Rep. 4 Ex. 273.

GLOSSARY

Advowson	The patronage of a Church benefice with the right of presentation.
Almuce	A fur hood and tippet worn by the clergy, different furs being worn to denote rank.
Bradishing	(Bratticing—archaic). The furnishing of castle ramparts with parapets, etc.
Cappa Nigra	Black cope with hood as worn by clergy in choir according to the Sarum use.
Compline	The office of the breviary said upon retiring at night.
Fellows	(In this context.) A member of a governing body of a college.
Hebdomadarius	In the Catholic Church, a member of a chapter whose week it is to officiate at the divine office.
Hide	A certain portion of land for the support of one family, from 18–20 acres.
Holy Orders	In the Catholic Church one who enjoyed the state of Bishop, priest, deacon (and formerly sub-deacon).
Knight's Fee	In English feudal law, a tenure of land held on condition of a knight's military service.
Lauds	The office sung at dawn in the Catholic Church containing psalms of praise (laudare).
Matins	The first of the hours of the Roman Breviary sung at midnight or just before lauds (Q.V.).
Misericord	A hinged seat in choir with a narrow ledge on the under side, which when turned up allowed one to rest while standing.
Moiety	One of two equal parts of an estate.
Mortmain	(Dead hand—old French.) The transfer of land or property to a corporate body, viz. Church or college.
None	The office of the Roman Breviary said at noon.
Ogee	An 'S'-shape curve forming a pointed arch.
Prime	The first of the day hours after lauds (Q.V.) according to the Roman Breviary.
Sext	One of the lesser hours of the Roman Breviary sung at the sixth hour (11 o'clock, taking 6.00 a.m. as the first hour).
Succentor	The assistant to the leader of a church choir, a 'precentor's' deputy.
Terce	The office sung at the third hour (viz. 8 o'clock, taking 6.00 a.m. as the first hour)
Tofts	A hillock, usually occupied by a dwelling house.
Vespers	(Vespres = evening, old French.) The office sung at eventide.
Vicaridy	The office or position of a vicar.

BIBLIOGRAPHY SOURCE MATERIAL

1. M. A. Tierney, *History and Antiquities of the Castle and Town of Arundel* (1834).
2. R. B. K. Petch, *The Organisation of a College of Secular Priests as Illustrated by the records of the College of the Holy Trinity, Arundel, 1380-1544* (Univ. of London unpub. M.A. Thesis) (1942).
3. J. Dallaway, *History of the Eastern Division of the County of Sussex* (1819), Vol. II, pt. 1, p. 166-174.
4. Sir William Dugdale (ed. Caley, etc.), *Monasticon Anglicanum* (1830), Vol. VI, pt. 3.
5. *V.C.H. Sussex*, Vol. 11, pp. 108-109 and 119-120.
6. V. H. St. John Hope, *On an Inventory of the goods of the Collegiate Church of the Holy Trinity, Arundel, taken 1st October 9 Henry VIII (1517) Archaeologia*, 2nd Series, Vol. XI (1908).
7. M. A. Tierney, *Notices connected with a recent excavation in the College Chapel at Arundel, Sussex Archaeological Collections* III, pp. 77-88.
8. E. A. Freeman, *The Case of the Collegiate Church of Arundel, Archaeological Journal*, XXXVII (1880), pp. 244-270.
9. C. F. Trower, *The Arundel Chancel Case, Sussex Archaeological Collections* XXX (1880), pp. 31-51.
10. *Dictionary of National Biography*.
11. G. E. Cockayne (ed.), sub. Arundel, *The Complete Peerage*.
12. M. D. Francis, *The Booklet of the Fitzalan Chapel, Arundel* (1931).
13. G. W. Eustace, *Arundel: Borough and Castle* (1922).
14. Charles Caraccioli, *The Antiquities of Arundel* (1760).
15. F. C. Allison, *The Little Town of Arundel* (1947).
16. Charles Thomas Stanford, *Sussex in the Great Civil War and the Interregnum 1642-1660* (1910).
17. F. W. Steer, *The Fitzalan Chapel, Arundel* (1974).

NOTES

Chapter I

1. R. B. K. Petch, *The Organisation of a College of Secular Priests as illustrated by the records of the College of the Holy Trinity, Arundel, 1380-1544* (Univ. of London unpub. M.A. Thesis) (1942), p. 1. *Cf. Domesday Book* f.422, '. . . the clerks of St. Nicholas hold 6 hides and there they have 6 villeins and 7 bórdars with 3 ploughs and so it was in the time of King Edward'.
2. M. A. Tierney, *History of Arundel* (London 1834), Vol. II, p. 578.
3. *Ibid.*, p. 575.
4. *Domesday Book, op. cit.*, f. 422.
5. M. A. Tierney, *op. cit.*, Vol. I, pp. 144-146.
6. *Ibid.*, Vol. II, p. 578.
7. *Ibid.*
8. *Ibid.*, p. 579.
9. F. C. Allison, *The Little Town of Arundel* (1947), p. 28.
10. M. A. Tierney, *op. cit.*, Vol. II, pp. 580-581.
11. *Ibid.*, pp. 583-585.
12. R. B. K. Petch, *op. cit.*, p. 4.
13. *Ibid.*, p. 5.
14. M. A. Tierney, *op. cit.*, p. 586.
15. *Ibid.*, p. 589-590.

Chapter II

1. M. A. Tierney, *History of Arundel* (London 1834), Vol. I, p. 49.
2. *Ibid.*, p. 591.
3. Statutes of Arundel College: vide supra, *op. cit.*, M. A. Tierney, Appendix No. VIII.
4. *The Complete Peerage*, ed. G. E. Cockayne, sub. Arundel (1910), p. 243.
5. *Cal. Papal Reg. 1. Papal petitions*, p. 81; *Bishop Grandison's Register*, ed. F. C. Hingeston-Randolph, p. 988.
6. (a) They were related in the 3rd and 4th degree, *The Complete Peerage, op. cit.*, p. 244; (b) The Papal mandate is dated 31 July 1347 on petition of the Earl's son, Edmund, who, with his two sisters, were subsequently declared illegitimate by the Bishop of Chichester. *Ibid.*, p. 244.
7. *Cal. Papal Reg., 1342-1362*, p. 176. *Bishop Grandison's Register, op. cit.*, p. 989.
8. *Ibid 1, petitions*, p. 99.
9. Preamble to Statutes of the College of the Holy Trinity, vide *op. cit.*, M. A. Tierney, Appendix No. VIII, p. 752.

10. (a) *Ibid*; (b) *Cal. Papal. Reg. Papal Letters III, 1342-1362*, p. 573.
11. Preamble to Statutes, *op. cit.*
12. R. B. K. Petch, *The Organisation of a College of Secular Priests as illustrated by the records of the College of the Holy Trinity, Arundel, 1380-1544* (Univ. of London, unpub. M.A. Thesis) (1942), p. 9.
13. Beaumont, Hautmont and Grossmont were names used to describe a keep on a mound vide, J. Dallaway, *Western Sussex*, Vol. II, p. 98.
14. *Ibid*.
15. *Ibid.*, p. 10.
16. M. A. Tierney, *op. cit.*, p. 595.
17. *Ibid.*, p. 596.
18. (a) *Cal. Patent Rolls, 1377-1381*, p. 151; (b) Herald to the Earl of Northampton, Richard Macheby appears to be the only one to hold this title: vide *London Survey: The College of Arms* (1963), p. 288.
19. *Ibid* p. 494.
20. M. A. Tierney, *op. cit.*, Appendix No. VII, p. 747.
21. *Ibid.*, p. 547.
22. *The Complete Peerage, op. cit.*, p. 238-239.
23. M. A. Tierney, *op. cit.*, p. 597.
24. R. B. K. Petch, *op. cit.*, p. 11.
25. M. A. Tierney, *op. cit.*, p. 548.
26. Dugdale *Monasticon Anglicanum*, Vol. VI, p. 1377.
27. Arundel Castle Archives, F.A. 9/MR3 RJ3.
28. R. B. K. Petch, *op. cit.*, p. 13. *Cf. Sussex Archaeological Collections*, V, p. 239.
29. M. A. Tierney, *op. cit.*, Vol. II, 'Notices of recent Excavation in the College Chapel at Arundel, *Sussex Arch. Coll.*, Vol. III, p. 10.
30. F. C. Allison, *The Little Town of Arundel* (1947), p. 28.

Chapter III

1. Dugdale, *Monasticon Anglicanum*, VI, p. 1379.
2. M. A. Tierney, *History of Arundel*, Vol. II, p. 600.
3. *Ibid.*, p. 598.
4. These are set out in Tierney, Appendix No. VIII.
5. Statutes, Cap. 7.
6. *Ibid.*, Cap. 9 and 10.
7. *Ibid.*, Cap. 9.
8. *Ibid.*
9. *Ibid.*, Cap. 12.
10. *Ibid.*
11. *Ibid.*, Cap. 13.
12. *Ibid.*, Cap. 10.
13. Almuce: a fur cape with tippets worn by clergy in choir, the quality of the fur denoting rank, *cf.* Anglican scarf.
14. R. B. K. Petch, *The Organisation of a College of Secular Priests as illustrated by the records of the College of the Holy Trinity, Arundel, 1380-1544* (Univ. of London unpub. M.A. Thesis) (1942), p. 15.

15. *Ibid.*, *cf.* Rushook's *Register*, f. 157.

Chapter IV

1. M. A. Tierney, *History of Arundel*, Vol. II, Appendix No. VIII, Cap. 3.
2. *Ibid.*, Cap. 9.
3. *Ibid.*, Cap. 2.
4. *Ibid.*, *loc. cit.*
5. *Ibid.*, Cap. 3.
6. *Ibid.*, *loc. cit.*
7. R. B. K Petch., *The Organisation of a College of Secular Priests as illustrated by the records of the College of the Holy Trinity, Arundel, 1380-1544* (Univ. of London unpub. M.A. Thesis) (1942), p. 107.
8. M. A. Tierney, *op. cit.*, p. 636.
9. R. B. K. Petch, *op. cit.*, pp. 160-161.
10. *Op. cit.*, p. 636.
11. R. B. K. Petch, *op. cit.*, pp. 163-164.
12. *Loc. cit.*
13. *Ibid.*, p. 167.
14. *Ibid.*, p. 168.
15. *Ibid.*, p. 169.
16. *Ibid.*, p. 173.
17. *Dictionary of National Biography.*
18. These Secular Canons differed from the older type of Collegiate foundations in not having canonries as freehold benefices.
19. The Masters of the College did not possess the cure of souls (Statutes Cap. 1), but were nevertheless beneficed.

Chapter V

1. M. A. Tierney, *History of Arundel*, Vol. II, p. 663.
2. *Ibid.*, p. 664.
3. *Ibid.*, p. 665.
4. *Ibid.*, p. 667.
5. This Leper Hospital may have stood outside the surviving old town gate on the north side (St. Mary's Gate) of the town where on the original London Road a gable end of a mediaeval building can be seen, incorporated into a stable building. Thus fulfilling the requirements of Leper Hospitals to be outside the town.
6. M. A. Tierney, *op. cit.*, p. 669.
7. *Ibid.*

Chapter VI

1. M. A. Tierney, *History of Arundel*, Vol. I, p. 241.
2. *Froissart's Chronicle*, Book. I, Cap. 336.
3. M. A. Tierney, *op. cit.*, p. 244.
4. *Froissart, op. cit.*, Book II, Cap. 49.

5. *Ibid.*

6. M. A. Tierney, *op. cit.*, p. 254. This proclamation is entered on the Rolls (III, 235), and establishes Arundel as the real leader of the confederate army.

7. *Dugdale's Baronage*, Vol. I, p. 319.

8. M. A. Tierney, *op. cit.*, p. 260. *Cf. Rot. Parl.*, III, p. 435.

9. *Complete Peerage*, ed. G. E. Cockayne, sub. Arundel, p. 244. A full account of his trial is given in the *Chronicle of Adam of Usk*. The church was destroyed by enemy action in 1940.

10. M. A. Tierney, *op. cit.*, p. 264. *Cf. Fabyan's Chronical*, II, p. 154.

11. Tichfield Cartulary, f. 107. *Cf.* Tierney, p. 267;

12. *Royal and Noble Wills*, 123–126. *Cf.* Tierney, p. 607.

13. There are three methods of numbering the Earls of Arundel. Disregarding the distinct creations, there were 24 Earls from Roger de Montgomery, who died in 1094, to Henry Fitzalan, who died in 1579/80. There were 19 Earls of the Aubigny and Fitzalan lines from William d'Aubigny, who died in 1176, to Henry Fitzalan, who died in 1579/80. Of the Fitzalans it is doubtful if the first two were ever Earls of Arundel, so if we regard Richard Fitzalan (died 1301/2) as the first of a new line, we have 12 earls beginning with him and ending with Henry, who died in 1579/80. No notice has been taken of the Earl of Kent and the Duke of Exeter, who were holders of the title after the executions of the 2nd and 4th Earls. Philip Howard, Earl of Arundel, who succeeded his maternal grandfather in the Castle and Honor of Arundel and died in 1595, was great-grandfather of Thomas Howard, Earl of Arundel, who was restored, in 1660, to the Dukedom of Norfolk as 5th Duke. The title was first created 29 September 1397, extinct in 1572 on the attainder of Thomas. 4th Duke of the Howard line. The present holder of the title is Miles, 17th Duke of Norfolk, C.B., C.B.E., M.C., 28th Earl of Arundel, Earl of Surrey and Norfolk, Baron Fitzalan, Clun, Oswaldestre and Maltravers, Earl Marshal and Hereditary Marshal of England. (*The Fitzalan Chapel, Arundel, a Guide and Short History*, F. W. Steer [1974], p. 4, footnote 2.)

Chapter VII

1. M. A. Tierney, *History of Arundel*, Vol. II, p. 606. *Cf.* Episcopal Register E., fol. 82.

2. *Ibid. loc. cit.*

3. *Ibid.*, p. 607.

4. *Ibid.*, p. 608. *Cf.* Episcopal Register C. 141, 1446, 1456.

5. *Ibid.*, p. 609.

6. *Ibid.*, p. 610.

7. *Ibid.*, p. 611.

8. R. B. K. Petch, *The Organisation of a College of Secular Priests as illustrated by the records of the College of the Holy Trinity, Arundel, 1380-1544* (Univ. of London unpub. M.A. Thesis) (1942), p. 18.

9. *Ibid. loc. cit.*

10. *Ibid.*

11. M. A. Tierney, *op. cit.*, p. 611.
12. *Ibid. loc. cit.*
13. Patent Roll. 36 Henry VIII, p. 21, m. 49.

Chapter VIII
1. G. W. Eustace, *Arundel: Borough and Castle* (1922), p. 151.
2. *Ibid. loc. cit.*
3. Charles Thomas Stanford, *Sussex in the Great Civil War and the Interregnum 1642–1660* (1910), p. 83.
4. M. D. Francis, *The Booklet of the Fitzalan Chapel, Arundel* (1931),
5. M. A. Tierney, *History of Arundel*, pp. 621–662.

Chapter IX
1. M. A. Tierney, *History of Arundel*, p. 613.
2. Catholic clergy were addressed as 'Mr.' at this date, only those in religious Orders being called 'Father'. Cardinal Manning introduced the modern custom of addressing all as 'Father'. However, the strong-minded northerners still persist with their 'Mr.' at Ushaw College, Co. Durham.
3. When the panels of the tabernacle were removed for restoration in 1937 the following note was discovered (12in. x 8in. approx.):
'This   T . . .rnacle was made by Chas. Kandler . . . smith att the miter In S^{t}martins Lane F . . . his Grace Thos Howard Du . . . Norfolk a . . .o Domonie 1730.'
(in smaller script add. note)
'The Tabernacle was cleaned and relined in 1848 when this paper was found, +, having been. mounted, to preserve it from further damage, was re-deposited in the place whence it was discovered. June 29. 1848.
—— Mark Tierney.
This Tabernacle may well be one of the first to be made in England after the Reformation.
4. A. MacCall, *The Church and Mission of St. Philip's Church, Arundel* (1906). MS. in Arundel Cathedral Archives.
5. *Ibid.*
6. *Ibid.*
7. *Arundel Cathedral Guide revised* (1978).

Chapter X
1. Philip M. Johnston, F.S.A., F.R.I.B.A., 'Poling and the Knights Hospitallers', *Sussex Archaeological Collections*, LXII, p. 95.
2. *Loc. cit.*, p. 95.
3. *Ibid.*, p. 94.
4. *Ibid.*, p. 96 (Canterbury Archiepiscopal Registers: Courtney, f. 208).
5. *Ibid.*, p. 96–98 (Lambert B. Larking, 'The Knights Hospitallers in England', Camden Soc. Series, pp. 24, 25. *Cf. V.C.H. Sussex* II, p. 93).
6. *Ibid.*, p. 94.

7. *Ibid.*, p. 86.

8. In a letter from Captain William Hemp of Lyminster House, Lyminster, to Dr. Eustace (author of *Arundel Borough and Castle*) dated 20 February 1914—in the possession of Miss E. G. Wedge of 34 Maltravers Street, Arundel.

Chapter XI

1. Francis C. Allison, *The Little Town of Arundel* (1947), p. 55.

2. It has been suggested that Lancastrians wore this collar of SS to signify their support of the Lancastrian claimant as the rightful 'sovereign'.

3. This was damaged during the 1939–45 War and removed for safety.

4. British Museum Harleian MS. 1076. John Withie, Herald Painter at the College of Arms.

5. Deposited in Arundel Cathedral archives.

6. Deposited in the Norfolk Estate Office, Arundel.

7. *St. Edmund, King and Martyr.*—St. Edmund was once the acknowledged patron of the English race as witnessed by the old shrine city of Bury St. Edmunds. The first English pilgrim hospice in Rome was dedicated to him, and all the English kings bore his banner into battle up to Edward I. On the Wilton diptych he is first in the line of English patron saints. (St. George was the official 'protector of the realm', but as personal patron of the sovereigns soon took precedence over Edmund.)

Between the years 1215 and 1217 Prince Louis of France was leading a punitive expedition against England in support of the barons against Henry III, but was defeated at the Battle of Lincoln in 1217. Before returning home, it is believed that he stole the relics of St. Edmund from his cathedral shrine and bore them off to France to even the score a little. The French today claim to have possessed the relics at the Church of St. Severin in Toulouse from 1219 to this day.

When Cardinal Vaughan was building Westminster Cathedral in 1901 he obtained, with papal permission, from Toulouse the body of St. Edmund to place in the new high altar (the French retaining the head). On 25 July the body was conveyed to the chapel of Arundel College to await transfer to Westminster Cathedral. Montague Rhodes James and other scholars of the day cast doubt on the authenticity of the relics, and Cardinal Vaughan asked the 15th Duke of Norfolk to keep them in the privacy of his private chapel in Arundel Castle. The French authorities proceeded to re-authenticate the head they still possessed, but the remains of the body were subsequently removed from the Castle chapel and placed in the vault near the high altar in the College chapel on 10 March 1971.

8. *St. Philip Howard.*—St. Philip Howard, 13th Earl of Arundel, was born at Arundel House in the Strand on 28 June 1557 and baptised in the Chapel Royal at Whitehall by Nicolas Heath, Archbishop of York, on 2 July 1557. His father was Thomas, 4th Duke of Norfolk, and his mother was the Lady Mary Fitzalan, daughter and co-heiress to Henry, 12th Earl of Arundel.

His father in siding with Mary Queen of Scots was attainted on 16 January (deprived of his honours and title) and beheaded on 2 June 1572; his mother died in the year of his baptism on 25 August 1557, a mere 17 years of age. Thus by 1570 Philip had succeeded to his maternal grandfather's title (his aunt, Joan, Lady Lumley, nee Fitzalan, having died without issue in 1576) as 13th Earl of Arundel, Lord Lumley, his uncle, having conveyed his life interest in the Castle and Honour of Arundel (*see* Additional Note).

Philip was educated at St. John's College, Cambridge, and soon embraced the life of a dashing, carefree, spendthrift courtier. Indeed, there is in the British Museum a manuscript account of his flirtation, after marriage, with one Mercy Harvey, a Puritan milkmaid. The chaste maid bad him consider his duty to God and his position, which quite chastened the young Earl. The nursery rhyme 'Where are you going to my pretty maid' fits the sequence exactly. *The Letter Book of Gabriel Harvey 1573-80*, ed. E. J. L. Scott, Camden Soc. Series, new series 33 (1884), pp. 143-158. *Cf.* Gabriel Harvey in *D.N.B.* Later overhearing Edmund Campion's defence of Catholicism he retired from Elizabeth I's court in 1584 and became reconciled to the Church of his baptism. This put him beyond the law and he was arrested the following year while trying to make his escape to the Continent. He spent the remaining 11 years of his life in the Tower. He was tried in 1589 for his reconciliation with the Catholic Church on a trumped-up charge of plotting against the queen, and was condemned to be hanged, drawn and quartered. He died before sentence could be carried out, on Sunday 15 October 1595, after suffering terrible privations, and was buried in a felon's grave (his late father's) in the crypt of the Tower Chapel of St. Peter ad Vincula.

There Philip's body remained until 1624 when his widow Anne, Countess of Arundel, petitioned King James I for its return. (The journey St. Philip's body took to Arundel is now the route of the Arundel Pilgrimage.) The mortal remains were encoffined in iron at West Horseley Place, where the countess lodged, and so conveyed to the ancestral vaults in the College Chapel at Arundel.

The years passed, and on 15 December 1929 Philip was beatified by Pope Pius XI, and on 25 October 1970 declared a Saint by Pope Paul VI. Thus on 10 March 1971 his remains were transferred from the College Chapel to a new shrine in the north transept of Arundel Cathedral, and the cathedral was re-dedicated to our Lady and St. Philip Howard in 1973.

Additional Note.—The claim to the earldom as being one by tenure of the Castle of Arundel was made by John Arundel, who had been summoned to parliament in 1429, the writ being directed 'Johanni Arundell "de Arundell" Chivaler'. In 1433 (11 Henry VI) he petitioned (as Earl of Arundel) to be summoned to parliament and considered as Earl of Arundel, a dignity or name united and annexed to the Castle and Lordship of Arundel, for time whereof memory of man was not to the contrary—a peculiar and distinct claim (as stated in the *First Report on the Dignity of a Peer*, p. 406), 'not connected with any general, but asserting a special right, and which being founded on prescription, was to be supported by evidence of constant and immemorial enjoyment of the asserted right, which right if not shown to have been so constantly enjoyed, the title by prescription failed. This claim, though opposed by John (Mowbray), Duke of Norfolk, was admitted by the Crown, not-withstanding that the assertion of the constant annexation of the title to the Castle of Arundel could not have been sustained, had it been (which it was not) made the subject of an enquiry'.

The claim then of 1433 was, as is stated above, 'admitted by the Crown, or so far admitted as that the assertion in the petition is made the consideration for the king's acceding to it, with a saving, nevertheless, of the right of the king, of the Duke of Norfolk (who, being a coh. of the Earls of Arundel, had opposed the earl's claim) and of every other person; which saving clause, as is remarked in the *First Report on the Dignity of a Peer*, "was that species of saving which is deemed in law illusory, operating nothing".' *See also* Tierney's *History of Arundel* (Vol. I, p. 106), where the judgment is set out, reciting 'that Richard Fitz Alan was seized of the Castle, Honour and Lordship [of Arundel] in fee; that, by reason of his possession thereof, he was without other reason or creation, EARL OF ARUNDEL, &c.'; and stating also, that 'the King, contemplating the person of the present claimant, now Earl of Arundel, &c., has, with the advice and assent of the Prelates, Dukes, Earls and Barons in this present Parl. assembled, admitted John, now Earl of Arundel, to the place and seat anciently belonging to the Earls of Arundel in Parl. and council'.

Almost similar words are used in the Act of Parliament obtained in 1627, which, in form of a petition to the king recites that the Earldom of Arundel had been real and that from the time whereof the memory of man was not to be contrary, and had, from the time aforesaid, been used and enjoyed by the petitioner and such of his ancestors as had possessed the Castle of Arundel, etc. Now it is to be noted that the claimant of 1433 alleged that his ancestors, the possessors of Arundel, were Earls of Arundel, both before, as well as after, the Conquest. Fortunately, however, King Harold and his father, Earl Godwin, have not to be included, and still less a long shadowy race of earls extending upwards towards (even if not including) primeval man. The words 'memory of man' must, of course, be read in their strict legal significance, as indicating the reign of Richard I, so that the Act of 1627 (and, possibly, the admission of 1433 also) would not apply to any Earl of Arundel, prior to 1189.

The Redesdale Committee remarks on these proceedings that they 'ought to be considered as an anomaly influenced by political views, and decided apparently without much discussion, and without the assistance of the Judges'. The assertion of fact by the claimant as to the earldom having always depended on possession of the castle in the past 'seems not to have been true, and not to have been made the subject of enquiry when the question was decided'. For a similar case of a charter creating a peerage, and setting out, as facts, unfounded statements of the grantee, *see* the Barony of LISLE, cr. 1444, in the same reign. (The Complete Peerage, sub Arundel.)

INDEX

Acolytes, 20
Act of Suppression, 39, 40
Addis, Joseph, 28
Adeliza, Queen, 2
Admiral of the English fleet, 33, 34
west and south, 33
Advent, 16
Alenson, John, 25
Alien priory, 4
Alltrop, John, 27
Almshouse, 29
Almsmen, 29, 30, 31.
Almuce, 19
Alps, 5
Angmering, 9, 14, 36
Ansty, Peter, 27
Aragon, 65
Arbuthnot, the Rev. George, 46
Arms, College of, 64
Arundel, Borough of, 2
Arundel Castle, 2, 7, 8, 9, 11, 13, 14, 17, 35, 36, 42, 47, 55, 58
private chapel, 66
Arundel Cathedral (of our Lady and St. Philip), 28, 48, 62, 67
Arundel Catholics, 28
Arundel College, 10, 11, 12, 13, 14, 15, 19, 27, 28, 29, 30, 33, 35, 36, 39, 40, 41, 42, 43, 47, 48, 49, 52, 53, 55, 71
Chantry College, 55
Master of, 10, 13, 14, 15, 16, 17, 18, 19, 20, 29, 36, 38
private oratory, 54
Arundel, Countess of (Anne Dacre), 62, 66

Arundel, Countess of (Eleanor Beaumont, see Beaumont).
(Eleanor Berkley), 22, 54, (see also Berkley)
(Joan Nevill), 63, 65, (see also Nevill)
Arundel, 1st Earl of, 2
2nd Earl of (Edmund), 7
3rd Earl of (Richard), 7, 8, 9, 14, 29, 33, 55, 65
4th Earl of (Richard), 9, 10, 11, 12, 14, 15, 16, 17, 19, 29, 31, 33, 34, 35, 36, 40, 52, 55, 56, 65
5th Earl of (Thomas), 31, 35, 55-58, 62, 65
6th Earl of (John), 22, 54, 58, 59, 65
7th Earl of (John), 58-59, 61, 65
8th Earl of (Humphrey), 59
9th Earl of (William), 22, 59, 60, 61, 63, 65
10th Earl of (Thomas), 39, 40, 60, 61, 65
11th Earl of (William), 40, 60, 61
12th Earl of (Henry), 40, 41, 47, 61, 66, 71
13th Earl of (Philip), see Howard, St. Philip
14th Earl of (Thomas), 42
Earl of (1st son of 15th Duke), 64
Earldom of, 2, 11, 55, 57
Earls of, 3, 7, 57, 59, 72
Arundel Mass, 60
parish of, 8
Priory, 2, 4, 5, 6, 7, 9, 10, 11, 12, 14, 16, 27, 49 (see also Arundel College)

114

Smythe, Adam, 24, 25
Sompting, 51
Soult, Adam, 23
Southampton, 5
South Harting, 1
South Stoke, 9, 14, 22, 36
Sovereign Order (*see* Malta)
SS, Collar of (Lancastrian), 57, 62
Statutes of the College, 15, 16, 19, 20
Stewart, infant daughter of Dr., 66
Storrington, 23
Steer, Francis, 66
Steward of Hospital, 30
Story, Bishop, 22
Strand, 61
Stratford, Robert, Bishop of Chichester, 5
Stubbar, John, 26
Sub-deacons, 20
Sub-master, 15, 16, 17, 18, 20
Succentor, 20
Suffolk, Earl of (Sir Michael de la Pole), 34
Sullington, 31
Surrey, Earldom of, 55
Sussex, 5
Sutton, 63

Teachford, Sir Richard, 42
Templar, Order of Knights, 51
Tewkesbury Abbey, 58, 59
Thanet, 33
Thom, Bernard, 28
Threele, John, 62, 65
Tichfield Abbey, 36
Tierney, The Rev. Mark, 21, 27, 44, 48, 59, 63, 66
Tompson, Christopher, 26
Tortington, 9, 14, 32, 36
Tower Hill, 35
Tower of London, 35, 57, 61 (Chapel of St. Peter ad Vincula), 62

Treasurer, Lord High, 57

Upmarden, 9, 36, 51
Venerable Order of St. John, 53
Vespers, 17
Vicar (at Arundel), 3, 46
Vicaridy, 3

Waldebef, John, 25
Waller, Sir William, 42, 43
Walsshman, John, 26
War Tax, 6
Warde (Wade), Robert, 27, 63, 65
Warham, William (Archbishop of Canterbury), 65
Warnham, 5
Warning Camp, 9, 14, 32, 36
Warwick, Earl of, 34, 60
Wells, Thomas, 26
Wepham, 9, 14, 36
Wepham, John, 25, 26
Westminster, 34, 35
Westminster Abbey, 60
White, John, 26
White, William (Master), 14, 21, 23, 24, 27, 63, 65
Widville, Margaret (*see also* Woodville), 65
Wilhelm II, Kaiser, 50
Winchester, 42
Winchester, Bishop of, 8
Winchester Cathedral, 58
Wingham College, Provost of, 22
Wisborough, 5
Withie, John, 64
Wolball, John, 25
Woodville, Margaret, 61
Wyltshire, John, 24
Wyndham, Philip, 28, 47

Yapton, 6
York Cathedral, 23
Yorkist emblem, 60, 63

LIST OF SUBSCRIBERS

Henry Baxby, O.St.J.
B. E. Billington, C.St.J.
Mrs. A. D. Botting
Sister Mary Camillus
D. Cavey
Miss Bridget Corbally
Stella Cresswell-Wall
Dr. E. C. Dawson
Peter Drummond-Murray
Mr. & Mrs. Paul Dunkley
R. M. Festing
Lady Winefride Freeman
Ena Mary Greenfield
R. G. Guest
H. M. Hammond
Miss Kathleen Harrison
T.W. Hendrick, F.R.S.A.
Sister Joan Henry
F. M. Hesketh
Peter F. Holland
Ronald Howell
S. Humphery
Cecil Humphery-Smith
Mrs. D. F. Joseph
Leonard V. Kemp
Christine Kenny
Elizabeth Kenny
James Kenny
Michael Kenny
Mr. and Mrs. J. de Landry
Kim C. Leslie
Colonel D. B. Long
Timothy J. McCann
Dr. Donald M. MacKay
Eileen Mahony
Sir Noel and Lady Moynihan

James R. Myerscough
Dr. K. W. Nicholls Palmer, C.St. J., T.D.
Major General The Duke of Norfolk,
  C.B., C.B.E., M.C., D.L.
Rev. Mother M. Paul
Mr. F. Penfold
Lady Rachel Pepys
Philip Perryman, F.R.I.C.S.
Lady Katherine Phillips
Ian Phipps
Raunds Nursing Division, St. John
A. H. Mordaunt Richards
Brigadier R. H. E. Robinson, C.B.E.,
  E.R.D.
Mrs. Ian Rodger
Robin Compigne Rogers
M. M. T. Rowe
Rev. Mother M. Scholastica
Mrs. A. G. Sharp-Paul
Frederick Shaw
F. W. Smith
Denis W. Stent
Nigel Stourton
E. Mary Sutton
B. J. F. Theobald, F.R.A.I., F.R.M.S.,
  A.A.S.I.
G. H. G. Tilling, O.St.J., M.A., F.S.A.,
  Scot.
Mrs. Janet Tippetts (S.E.N.)
Bruce Todd
Peter Townsend
Jeanne Wall
The Revd. Michael Weaver (Vicar of
  Arundel)
West Sussex Record Office
Mr. & Mrs. John Wiseman